ENDORSEMENTS

"**Million Dollar Soup** by author Janet-Lynn pairs the power of personal exploration with the recipe for transforming ideas and thoughts into reality. She invites the reader to dream without limits and expand their realm of possibility by creating even bigger opportunities in one's life."

- Judy O'Beirn,
President of Hasmark Publishing International

Janet-Lynn masterfully creates a simple, comprehensive guide for achieving happiness and fulfillment through an insightful analogy to the preparation of a simple bowl of soup, which she transforms seamlessly into the preparation of a tantalizing and rewarding lifestyle.

- Gary Aitken, retired Trent University professor
and co-author of three editions of "Arriba,"
the first introductory Spanish program
for Canadian beginners

Within the pages of this book, Janet-Lynn shares her discoveries with you, drawing directly from her own life's personal challenges and experiences and combining them with her passionate interest in personal development and growth. She strives to inspire others, as she herself has been inspired, to rise above conflicts and self-doubt, to a life filled with peacefulness and purpose. Through steady analogy of transforming a common bowl of soup into an unforgettable taste experience, she takes you on a highly relatable journey to your own ultimate destination of serenity and empowerment.

- Peter Noce, producer
and host of 'The Sill' podcast

"'The Million Dollar Soup' is a wonderful, uplifting, inspiring and an incredibly, uniquely-written book, full of amazing ideas. I could not put it down. This book is wisdom and solace for all ages. The world needs storytellers to help us rise up from the chaos and fear of these interestingly complex times. We need to hear stories that awaken us and inspire us to take action to change and live to the fullest. Janet-Lynn has created the million-dollar idea, a recipe for happiness and prosperity, insights that anyone can use to improve any part of his or her life. I am in love with personal self-growth and this fantastic book is a powerful reminder that main ingredients are the gifts that came free with us when we were born, ones we cannot purchase but can access any time. Ingredients that will change our life for the better, if we choose to use them. Absolutely a must read for all."

- Vladimira Kuna,
International Bestselling Author

"Janet-Lynn's 'The Million Dollar Soup' is a true feast for the senses. Her powerful concepts provide the reader with the tools and knowledge to embrace the transformative power that lies within us all. Be prepared to embrace transformation in your life, and discover a book that will stick with you for years to come."

- Ana Parra Vivas,
International Bestselling Author of '*I Trust My Inner Voice*'

Janet-Lynn Morrison's new book, Million Dollar Soup, is quite simply 'delicious'. The metaphors she uses apply as perfectly to our lives as they do to the insights gained from our experiences. Janet-Lynn has whipped up a scrumptious mix of practical guidance and understanding that only comes from consciously living through the ebbs and flows of life.

Far more than just a recipe, you can think of this book as an intuitive fast track to help you cook up your very own Million Dollar Soup.

- Dave Falle, Technical Writer

"A perfect life does not exist, but a happy and successful one certainly can. In Janet-Lynn Morrison's, *The Million Dollar Soup: A Recipe for a Meaningful Life,* she takes the reader on an inspiring journey through a series of heartfelt stories that reveal how she has learned to do just that. As she chronicles the traumatic events that could possibly have destroyed her, Janet-Lynn reveals the one common thread that was ever-present throughout her lifelong struggles. It was a simple bowl of soup. She recounts how soup has always had, for her, a healing quality, something that not only filled her body, but filled her soul as well. It became the catalyst that has energized her toward positive action, and ultimately allowed her to reach her full potential. It has become her recipe for her *own* meaningful life.

"Through this page-turning book, the author shows us in disarming detail that *The Million Dollar Soup* is not about money. It's about a mindset. It's a mentality, a metaphor upon which to build a meaningful life. Janet-Lynn shows us in intricate detail how you can achieve your dreams, so you too can *FEEL* like a million dollars.

"This book is about making your *own million-dollar soup*! It represents your purpose, your goals, your aspirations. The soup is your segue through which you can put your ideas into action, to clear the way to achieve happiness and ultimate success. You *ARE* "The Soup".

"*The Million Dollar Soup* is truly a thought-provoking and inspirational read!"

- Caryn Nash,
Bestselling Author of *Legacies of Love*

THE MILLION-DOLLAR SOUP

A Recipe for a Meaningful Life

by

Janet-Lynn Morrison

Hasmark Publishing
www.hasmarkpublishing.com

Copyright © 2022 Janet-Lynn Morrison

First Edition
No part of this book may be reproduced or transmitted in any form or by any means, electronic or mechanical, including photocopying, recording or by any information storage and retrieval system, without written permission from the author, except for the inclusion of brief quotations in a review.

Disclaimer
This book is designed to provide information and motivation to our readers. It is sold with the understanding that the publisher is not engaged to render any type of psychological, legal, or any other kind of professional advice. The content of each article is the sole expression and opinion of its author, and not necessarily that of the publisher. No warranties or guarantees are expressed or implied by the publisher's choice to include any of the content in this volume. Neither the publisher nor the individual author(s) shall be liable for any physical, psychological, emotional, financial, or commercial damages, including, but not limited to, special, incidental, consequential or other damages. Our views and rights are the same: You are responsible for your own choices, actions, and results.

Permission should be addressed in writing to Janet-Lynn Morrison at jjlmorrison@gmail.com

Editor:
Cover Design: Anne Karklins anne@hasmarkpublishing.com
Interior Layout: Amit Dey amit@hasmarkpublishing.com

ISBN 13: 978-1-77482-175-6
ISBN 10: 1774821753

DEDICATION

To all of you beautiful souls who valiantly chase your dreams while holding onto the unwavering belief that anything is possible.

"LIVE IMPOSSIBLY"

- JANET-LYNN MORRISON

ACKNOWLEDGMENTS

To those of you who have stood by me and cherished me along my journey, never wavering in your belief that my dreams would someday become a reality.

CONTENTS

Foreword xiii

Introduction: A Recipe for Life xv

Chapter 1: Be Water: *The Driving Force of All Nature* 1

Chapter 2: Understanding Flavors: *Discovering Your Purpose and Mission* 15

Chapter 3: Evaluating Your Measurements: *Creating Balance in Your life* 31

Chapter 4: A Dash of Salt: *Recognizing Adversity with a Grain of Salt* 49

Chapter 5: A Pinch of Rock Bottom: *How I Rebounded, and So Can You* 61

Chapter 6: Three Cups of Strength and a Dash of Empathy: *Perseverance, Determination, and Endurance* 73

Chapter 7: Don't Forget to Stir: *Motion Creates Successful Stability* 85

Chapter 8: Two Tablespoons of Positive Thinking: *The World Rewards Confidence* 95

Chapter 9: Keep Stirring: *Nothing Comes Easy* 109

Chapter 10: Leave to Simmer: *You Have What You Need; Now What Do You Want?* 121

Chapter 11: Now What? *Let's Get Cooking!* 137

About the author 151

FOREWORD

In 'A Million Dollar Soup,' the author skillfully stirs together timeless ingredients of wisdom, personal experience, and profound insights, offering readers a recipe for a life rich with purpose and joy. The culinary-themed chapters are more than a delightful play on words; they act as a metaphor, guiding readers through a meticulously crafted recipe to craft a life of substance and fulfillment. Each chapter adds a unique flavor, a new depth to the understanding of what it means to live a life of meaning, with every lesson presented being a necessary ingredient in the grand scheme of personal development.

From learning to navigate life's adversities with a 'grain of salt' to understanding the power of positive thinking and confident living, the book encourages readers to actively participate in the conscious creation of their life story. It emboldens them to stir, simmer, and season their personal journey to perfection.

Whether you find yourself at 'rock bottom' or on a steady simmer, this book offers you the essential ingredients to enrich your life's broth with resilience, understanding, and purpose. It doesn't just stop at guiding you to find all you need; it pushes you to think about what you want, instilling a profound belief that the right blend of determination, positivity, and balanced living can indeed yield a life that is both meaningful and richly rewarding.

'A Million Dollar Soup' is more than just a book; it's a nurturing mentor, a beacon of wisdom guiding you towards a pathway of enriched living. It's a warm, wise, and invigorating read, a perfect companion for anyone yearning to live a life flavored with purpose, joy, and fulfillment."

Peggy McColl, New York Times Best-Selling Author
http://PeggyMcColl.com

Please let me know if you have any questions!!

INTRODUCTION

A RECIPE FOR LIFE

There I was, standing in my kitchen, stirring the boiling pot of a luscious, homemade soup that I had just made, complete with all of my very special ingredients. The aroma was mesmerizing, seductive in a sense. I could already feel the warmth of the liquid coursing through my entire body, creeping through every crevice and warming it to the core. As the aroma traveled to my nose, I could feel my senses awakening. Then, as I sipped a spoonful of the succulent liquid, I was overcome by a remarkable idea.

Soup, just like life, is a combination of several ingredients that harmoniously work together to create a wonderful experience, one that leaves you feeling satisfied, content, and happy. If we regard soup as a metaphor for life, then we might begin to better understand how our decisions, actions, and, of course, ingredients that are ever-present, work to give us either a bowl full of satisfaction or leave us feeling remarkably empty.

At one time or another, we have all experienced the warmth, fulfillment, and nourishment of a big bowl of soup. For many young children, soup is one of the first experiences they'll have with food. As you grow, soup becomes comforting, a healing agent when you are sick, a means to warm your body when it's cold, and an easy food to cook, eat, and store. Soup dates to ancient times. It's one of the most basic and fundamental building blocks of our ancestors' diets.

Soup for me, as well, has been an important staple throughout my life. But now I have begun to think about it in a different light—not just as a delicious and delectable meal, but also as a symbol for our entire lives. Soup, just as with life, has several ingredients. Some may be indispensable… essential to the flavor, while others may be accent notes. In life, you clearly have pillars and crucial ingredients: your family, your profession, your faith. Plus, all those added extras that complement them: your lifestyle, your education, your principles.

Just like in your soup, the ingredients in your life add flavor and zing or they can undermine the other flavors. With soup, as with anything else, make sure you add just the right amount of flair. Remember, even though some recipes are passed down, yours are unique, and it's up to you to inform your audience how you concocted your million-dollar soup.

Like life, soup comes in several temperatures. Think about how hot soup might taste right out of the pot. You don't want to eat it, as it would probably burn you. That can represent the challenges we face throughout life. However, if you wait too long, the soup gets cold, representing the notion of waiting too long—missed opportunities. And, of course, sometimes the temperature of the soup is just right, reminding us of the perfect and wonderful moments of life, those we cherish the most.

Soup can be as varied as the stars in the sky. Thousands of soup recipes exist, exemplifying the remarkable intricacies, depth, and options life often presents us. Choosing your soup ingredients is like making choices in life. Some will be complementary and end with a great soup, while others may fall flat and require adjustment or reconsideration.

A hearty soup always consists of a wide selection of ingredients that have been simmering and marinating, and other soups may have just begun their preparation by mixing with other ingredients in the pot. No matter where you are in your journey as the soup chef, you will always find that the most flavorful soup is one that has been tried and tested. We have all heard the saying: "Variety is the spice of life."

In short, soup mirrors life in the sense that they both are the sum of the ingredients you introduce into them. And so, if you are going to make soup, then I want to help you make *a million-dollar soup*. That is the perfect, no-nonsense, soul-warming, deep-diving, save-the-leftovers-for-tomorrow kind of soup. It will be abundant, prosperous, and all-around wonderful. In this book, we will learn how to carefully plan our recipe, choose the best ingredients, focus on our preparation, remain patient, and eventually create something fantastic. But it will not be easy, and it won't come without challenges.

Today, lots of us take the path of least resistance. That is like soup in a can. It's easy, but it's not all that great. But the easy way is not always the best choice. It's too simple. In a metaphorical sense, it's akin to allowing society its right to conform, with everyone following like sheep.

But sometimes making canned soup is where you have to start. I remember eating canned soup as a child, and for me, mushroom soup was the worst. It was a congealed, stiff, gelatinous substance. That was never soup, was it? As a matter of fact, canned soup only becomes malleable when you put the heat on, and that's when the transformation occurs, and canned soup becomes edible. It's the same with us; we will never know what change is unless we feel the heat. This book is here to show you how to keep cool when the heat is on!

Each day presents a series of tests, and a mixture of good and bad things may happen. You can't predict how you may react to any of them. Fight or flight, a well-known behavioral response, kicks in. We can simply cower and hope the problem goes away, or we can react and deal with the situation head on. I choose the route of the warrior. I become the king or queen of my realm and treat every day with the same determination, regardless of how many times I fall or who kicks me when I'm down. Just like you, I'm the product of my life's work, the person I've become after every fall and kick. I learned to kick right back even when pinned to the ground. No single, specific experience led me to be who I am today. It was an accumulation of all the little life events I have experienced. I want to inspire you to get in touch with your own warrior spirit as it's an important ingredient in your life's soup.

Another crucial component of your soup is deciding what you want to make. This is your purpose and will become the base of your soup. Make a choice and never stop working on it, no matter what gets in your way. Then choose your ingredients wisely. Don't be afraid to experiment. Make sure to add ingredients that will make your soup and your life unique: failure, tears, heartache, love, pain, perseverance, determination, kindness, emotion, and dedication. They all play a crucial role. Just like seasoning, they will help you find the right balance.

Then continue adding ingredients. Never stop adding them. Take stock, taste it, add more, change things up, try something new, make adjustments. You will love some of them, and others, not so much.

I have experienced so many struggles over my lifetime and the lessons that I've learned could fill an entire book. And it was through this realization that the idea of my million-dollar soup was born.

So here I am, sharing how these experiences have helped me create and oftentimes re-create myself, each time better than the "me" of before. Because life changes us. We can never stand still. In my life, I have experienced enough to fill multiple lifetimes. Through those experiences I've developed strength, resilience, ferocity, and tenacity. But most importantly, I have developed competence because my experiences led me to become the best I can be. I've made my million-dollar soup over and over again, learning from my mistakes along the way. I have had to start from scratch so many times that I now know which ingredients work, and which ones don't. Nonetheless, each experience moves me forward and I can safely say that I'm very comfortable with who and where I am in my life right now.

Everything I have been through is a testimony to who I am today and that is why I can help teach you to use your own experiences to form a recipe for your best, empowered self.

Nothing will stand in your way when you become this person. I believe you can accomplish whatever you set out to do. As I write this book, I'm testifying to my own words because I'm creating my own million-dollar soup. The soup is never done, and this book is just another ingredient, because once it's written it will keep evolving. Once you read it, yours, too, will change!

Your soup is your life. It doesn't matter how many ingredients you have. Rather, what matters is your belief in yourself right now. If you have ever made soup, you know that all you need is a little bit of water and a couple of ingredients. It may not be the best soup, but you're on your way. Now, carefully choose the ingredients that you have on hand and add more, if necessary. And of course, you will need time. Even when that soup seems like it's ready, it may not be. You must taste it and determine whether or not you need to cook it more, change its flavor or even start a new soup.

It's all about choosing the right ingredients, and then believing in yourself, no matter what others may tell you. We are all capable of making the best version of our own million-dollar soup, our metaphor for becoming successful in life. Once we succeed, we are destined to live the life of our dreams, a life we created one wonderful recipe at a time.

I have been experimenting with many life-soup recipes throughout the different stages in my life, most of which contain some or all the ingredients included in the list below. But don't restrict yourself to only these ingredients. Feel free to add your own! As I realized over time, you may need to mix it up, make different combinations, or even throw some away and start from scratch. It's your soup, your life!

Here are some of the ingredients for my million-dollar soup.

- Adventure
- Ambition
- Athlete
- Art
- Author
- Business Owner
- Compassion
- Competition
- Confidence
- Confusion
- Daring
- Defiance
- Determination
- Discovery
- Education
- Empathy
- Exercise
- Failure
- Family
- Fitness
- Forgiveness
- Friendship
- Gratitude
- Grief
- Grit
- Guilt
- Healing
- Heartache
- Hope
- Illness
- Joie de vivre
- Joy
- Laughter
- Love
- Marriage
- Meditation
- Motherhood
- Music
- Opposition
- Optimism
- Perseverance
- Resilience
- Resourcefulness
- Rock Bottom
- Sadness
- Sassiness
- Self-awareness
- Sports
- Strength
- Stubbornness
- Survival
- Sweat
- Tenacity
- Travel

Start mixing them together and let them simmer for a while. Then slowly increase the heat as you add some hope and determination, allowing the delectable flavors to unite and soothe your soul.

With my own recipes, I experienced that they improved over time. My own list of *core ingredients* grew larger as my life unfolded, and the true flavors of my life were discovered. I was able to recognize other ingredients and introduce them lovingly into the fold, just as easily as I discarded others. I'm truly grateful for each new discovery that I managed to add to my special recipe, and which enabled me to grow. I will never stop learning and will continue to change up those ingredients and they, too, will become the catalysts to my growth. Robin Sharma, a Canadian litigation lawyer, and the writer of "Mega Living" (1994), a book on stress management and spirituality, said that "change is hard at first, messy in the middle, and gorgeous at the end!" It's time to grab your pot, pull up those sleeves, and get messy! I look forward to sharing my next recipe with you!

Read on and prepare yourself for your own delicious million-dollar soup. But before you dig into the next pages, for a few minutes, turn your attention away from what you *think* the metaphor for a million-dollar soup is and come with me on an exploration of how I combined different recipes to create the perfect million-dollar soup, or what I call *life*! You will find that some ingredients in my story will be sour, some sweet, some bitter, some salty, and some scrumptious—but most of all they will be *real*. From raw ingredients to cooked, my soups have become a metaphor for my life, and in the following pages, my hope is that you will find your new world of freshness, vibrancy, and authenticity.

This book is the HEAT you need to release the remarkable flavors and ingredients of your own life. It's not difficult and is easily repeated if you simply understand and choose your ingredients wisely. By doing so, in combination with the following pages, you will give yourself all that you need to build the flavors, generate the warmth, and experience great joy in its purest form.

It's your soup, your life! Good luck and enjoy your meal!

CHAPTER 1

WATER:
THE DRIVING FORCE OF ALL NATURE

Empty your mind; be formless, shapeless, like water.

– Bruce Lee

Life without purpose is like soup without water. Without water, your concoction isn't soup. Sure, you may have all the other ingredients, such as vegetables, proteins, spices, and so on, but it's just a bunch of items thrown together in a pot.

Life is like that too. You may have all of the other *ingredients* in your life, such as a nice home, a healthy relationship, good family, and loving friends, but these *ingredients* aren't enough if you can't otherwise find *fulfillment* through a *purpose*.

Water has become, throughout my journey, the *base* of my *soup*. It symbolizes the *foundation*... the *purpose* of my *life*. Without a *purpose*, one cannot find meaning and subsequent *success*.

So how do you find your *purpose*? The universe doesn't simply reveal it to you when it feels you are ready. Rather, it's up to you to *choose* your *purpose*. It's *your* choice, whether you are five or a hundred and five. Only *you* can determine your goals, your true *purpose* in life. You must set out and discover your own path. Too many people spend their lives *thinking* about their dreams and not *living* them. *Choices* are what make us whole and provide a path toward *self-completion*. Can you imagine how boring your life would be if every single step in your life were carved out for you? You would be submerged in a saltless, baseless, flavorless soup, with an insipid mind with no zing. Having *choices* automatically gives you *freedom*, and in this you can become the architect of your life and start to see your destiny precisely how you imagine it!

Even though most soups will have *water* as the base, you might decide that, for your soup, you will also add cream or a stock to the base. It's up to us to decide what is right for our own soup and our own lives. Once you choose the *base* for your soup, i.e., your *purpose* in life, the other ingredients will more easily fall into place. As your soup begins to cook, the flavors will blend and create a treasure of your life.

The *water* in soup is much like the *foundation* of a house. All houses start from the ground up. They might all have a front door, some windows, a roof, and similar rooms within, but they are different. Just as there are infinite possibilities and variations when you are building a house, it's the same with your soup. You may want a solarium in your home. Likewise, you may decide on chicken rather than vegetable stock in your soup. And the same is true of all the other components you decide to include in your house or your soup. Your *purpose* may be modified as you change or add to it.

No *possession* can create lasting happiness like a definite *purpose* can. How do you think successful people get to where they are? Their soup doesn't consist of only dry ingredients; the *base* is *water!* The *water*, or their *purpose*, fills the whole pot. They allow everything else to add flavor to their base and complement it but never overpower it.

Success in life begins with a *purpose*. You may have a loving marriage, or a dream home, but these things cannot create lasting fulfillment. However, when you add *purpose* to the pot, all the other components of your life become aligned. When you obtain that sports car with the money from the hard work that you put toward it, then your sports car is a perfect addition to your soup. When that dream home becomes your sanctuary, you may need a bigger pot to hold your soup. Water is certainly the flow of life, and, knowing that our *beliefs* and body composition are made up of 70% water, it's safe to say that our flow of life begins with a base for our dreams. Create the flow toward consistency and you will see your *million-dollar soup* flourish to new heights!

Water as the Base

Just as every soup starts with water, every life starts with a strong base on which to build. Most soups begin with cold or room-temperature water which you then warm with heat. You eventually add ingredients to develop the flavor, just as you choose different lifestyles and different ingredients for your life. Again, you might want to add chicken stock, or maybe beef or vegetable. Each of us has a uniqueness that is our own, like the flavor of our original soup. You add the elements that make you, you. If we don't add anything to the water, it will never become a soup. Just as, if we never add purpose to our lives, we will remain unfulfilled, always on the lookout for that special, yet sometimes illusive, ingredient. Ingredients add flavor to our soup and, in our lives, combine with our purpose to become the essence of who we are and how we choose to live our lives.

For most of us, water is merely something that we add to our pot, but there is something very special about water. It's everywhere. As Hermann Hesse wrote in *Siddhartha*: "But of all the water's secrets, he saw today only a single one, one that struck his soul. He saw that this water flowed and flowed, it was constantly flowing, and yet it was always there; it was always eternally the same and yet new at every moment! Oh, to be able to grasp this, to understand this!"

The First Step: Put It In The Pot

In the process of making soup, *water* is the odorless, flavorless recipient of a variety of *ingredients*. Think of the *water* as being akin to your *mind*, the foundation of your *life*. The *ingredients* you add to the *water* represent your *life purposes, goals,* and *dreams*. *Water* offers you the instrument that you need in order to navigate through your *life* as you add *ingredients* along the way.

However, the introduction of *ingredients* (your *purposes*) into the *water* (your *mind*) only begins the process. At this point there is no *action*. You need to add *heat* in order to move toward converting your *purposes* into reality. The introduction of *heat* makes the *water's* molecules move faster, and as you turn up the *heat*, you put your *ingredients* (*purposes*) into motion and move more closely towards *tasting* your prepared *soup* (i.e., *reaching* your *goals* and *dreams*).

Flavors are akin to your *belief system*. By adding ingredients, you are tasting... testing the waters. You are in charge, empowered to make whatever and, as many, soups as you wish, adjusting each one along the way. Think of these variations as the different facets of your life to which you are deeply dedicated. Once you reach your goal, select another facet and make a new soup. Each new recipe represents a new or different, flavorful moment in *my* life, as I embarked on new beginnings. Never be afraid to start something new! The fresh *stimulation*, and the engaging *anticipation* of the application and reward of your new dream will inspire you to pick up the *heat* and keep moving. As with soup, heat acts as the *stimulant* and this is where *passion* is undeniably awakened from its dormant state. Get ready to feel the flow!

Sadly, so many people never get around to *truly* making their soup. They may pour the water in, add a few ingredients, and then feel satisfied that the soup is ready. We see this in our everyday lives. We all experience it. We set out to accomplish a goal and stop because we experience failure, or it's too uncomfortable or difficult to continue. Perhaps we then restart it several times, unsure of what to add next. We find ourselves without a recipe or plan of action. We are hoping someone will come along and *make it for us* or be the magic solution to our problem while we remain uncertain of how to do it ourselves. And amid this confusion, we become bamboozled, like a dog chasing its tail round and round. We get things done but not in the way we think they ought to be. We never stop to make a list and select the right ingredients. And this is where a mentorship, or a Michelin-star chef comes in to assist you with your soup, to help you attain your vision. A mentor can help you move forward and can give you the drive and gusto to see your *own* potential. A mentor is not there to provide an easy fix, but rather is someone who can ensure that all the miraculous parts of you are highlighted.

Giving up can be so easy, and sometimes the ingredients you choose are all wrong and your soup misses the mark. You realize they are not connecting, so you give up. You try another person's soup and feel bitter and jealous that their version is so wonderful while yours doesn't even exist. You may even believe their soup came easily, that they had better ingredients available to them. These limiting beliefs can stop us dead in our tracks. They are nonstarters and prevent growth and the wonderful experience of a fully curated, delicious pot of soup.

Even if you have never made soup before, you can certainly make some now. All you need is to decide to believe in yourself. Be determined to make a soup that satisfies you, one that you can be proud to serve up to the world. Dare to be bold, be unique and try something new. Change the course of your life by opening your mind to its possibilities. By tapping into your goodness and taking responsibility for the person you were meant to be, you will unlock the ingredients for your soup. Don't worry! You can make it a little different every time. Just follow your stomach and sense of taste. This will lead you to the right recipe. Think of an ingredient you would like to add to your life. For example, a new hobby, a new social setting, a new environment. Knowing that your energy is in constant motion gives you the space to always evolve and re-create yourself. I can't begin to tell you how many times I have felt like a chameleon… shifting, changing, and becoming completely present and aware of the moment.

When you begin to cook, you are taking responsibility for your life and for the person you will become. When you mess up and fail, don't give up. Just re-boot, start over. You can do it. Some people may not like it and say it's all wrong. Don't listen! Follow your gut. As humans, we have been given this incredible gift, *life*. What are we going to do with it? Conform and live a mediocre life? Or find our purpose and live our dreams? What makes you feel alive? What matters most to you? The sound of music, how you feel when you run, the aroma of a special meal cooking in the oven, the joy of going barefoot in the grass, the crash of ocean waves against your body? Whatever it is, pursue it without stopping. Be relentless.

Water should be an example to us all. It's fluid, moving around obstacles that stand in its way, such as a large rock in the middle of a flowing river. It simply navigates around it or over it. It never stops. The same should be true for you and your life. Keep moving. If you truly wish to accomplish something amazing, be hungry. Don't become sidetracked by others and obstacles. Saddle up and get going!

We all have the ability to create our own life, the recipe for our soup. In the following pages, I will help you to accomplish just that. Everyone has a different soup, and we can choose the ingredients we want to put in it. *Water*, as its base, symbolizes our *life's purpose*, what we need to sustain ourselves and make ourselves whole. We all need and want something different, whether it's to go to school, graduate, find a job, get married, buy a house, have kids, and then retire. Nothing wrong with that! Or you may want to invent something new, travel the world, build a village in a Third World country. So, if you want to add milk, cream, flour, or something else to your base, that's okay too. Why? Because it's your *soup*, your *life*.

Water Is Foundation

We are creatures of free will in a society that has set out an imaginary blueprint for each of us to follow. But instead of doing that, we should embody our own unique design. No two people are identical, just as no two tastes are identical. The ingredients that make up your life ARE different from everyone else's. Your purposes are unique to you. They will change throughout your life, as will your soups.

Remember, *water* is the foundation to *soup* much like your *mind* is the foundation to *life*. Once you choose your *purpose*, the other ingredients can start mixing, creating a unique flavor for your soup. Stop the chatter before it gets into your head. Stop now and think. Why have you been holding back? What have you always wanted to do but didn't because you thought you couldn't do it? What are your dreams? Everyone was born with a *purpose*; it's up to you to decide what it is.

You must work with your *mind* to discover your dreams and self-reflect: What thoughts keep recurring? What excites you? What gets you out of bed ready to jumpstart your day instead of pressing the snooze button? Les Brown, a renowned motivational speaker, described that his life's mission was to inspire people to live their purpose, and he touched millions. Initially he thought his purpose was to be a disc jockey. As he pursued his dream, he became laser-focused and began to align with his true purpose. We are all here to serve humanity and improve our world. No one knows what another person can do. There are no limits. You need to break out of your mold, your robotic-like routine. You need to relinquish mediocrity and go for the best! Don't allow the gifts you were given to die within you. Let yourself shine and become an example of what is possible.

Have you noticed how naturally good you are at some things? And when you are engaging in those activities you get lost in them? You love it. Well, there is a very good chance that this is your *purpose*. We can often get caught up in the path of working, making money, buying things, going places, having experiences. We are so focused on *getting* instead of *giving*, and in just *doing* that we lose our *purpose*. The talents and abilities we were born with wither away until they are no longer there.

Consider young children. Don't you love how they believe anything is possible? They haven't really *done* much of anything yet, and they don't know anything about time or the future. They are only interested in the *now*, and everything they do is new to them. They are always imagining new identities, adventures, and friends for themselves. A magical unicorn? A superhero who sees through walls? A dragon slayer? An adorable puppy? Children are fascinating! They are not thinking about boundaries, about rules, or what others will think of them. We have a lot to learn from these little humans and should attempt to nurture their imaginations and dreams so that they can live their lives experiencing the joy of their own genius.

The best part about discovering your *purpose* is the effect this has as it trickles down into every aspect of your life, just as adding *ingredients* to your soup creates texture and richness. Perhaps your purpose is something completely different from what you thought it to be, but nonetheless, it's yours to decide. That is the beauty of life. Be who you were destined to be, in your dreams, as a child, when you imagined yourself as the most flawless version of yourself, living your passion, not what somebody else wants you to be. Choose your greatest passion, the biggest part of what makes you tick, just like the beat of a melody.

Be proud and stand up for who you are and for who you are becoming. You will begin attracting all kinds of good things. Health, wealth, happiness, and joy can be within your reach with ease, bliss, and most of all, consistency. You can be richer than you ever dreamed possible. Life can become truly magnificent. Your *purpose* will be the one thing that holds you together on difficult days and, most likely, the reason behind all the good days.

Think about the *purpose* of each *ingredient* in your soup and what it adds, so that you have a better understanding. Then you can decide to leave it out or you can replace it with something else. Most ingredients will add flavor, but some also serve another function, such as flour, which may serve as a thickener in a sauce.

Some *ingredients* are foundational and can't be removed or omitted, such as hard work, tenacity, dedication, honesty, and pride. Remove any one of them and your *soup/life* will be different from what you are hoping for. One way to sort out which ingredients are foundational to your *soup/life* is to think, self-reflect, read, and educate yourself.

Henry Ford once said, "Thinking is the hardest work there is," which is probably the reason why so few people engage in it." Are you thinking? I mean, *really* thinking. Many people think they are, but the truth is only 1% of people actually *do* think, 4% *think* they think, and 95% would rather *die* than think. So, which one are you? Maybe you are *overthinking* everything, especially now, and you've thought yourself into a corner. Maybe you are prone to decision paralysis that has you stuck in a loop of procrastination. "Oh, I'll start tomorrow. I'll start Monday. Umm, maybe next week, next month, next year. I'll wait until my birthday, after Christmas, when I have the right haircut, when the summer's over…when I have more resources…" But what if that day doesn't come? We all have the ability to think, and thus create meaningful, new experiences, and reach our goals, but the one thing we don't have a lot of is *time*. Life is happening now. We don't know how long we are going to be here. So why not start *today*?

Pick an idea/dream that you want to make a reality and consider writing down your recipe. Arrange all the ingredients in the order you feel would lead to the best result and then outline the steps you need to take. Ask yourself which steps are essential and which ones you can omit or use later. Are any of the steps overlapping or unnecessary? Recipes are like art. Become the chef you have always dreamed of being and create a soup that will expand your life and make you successful.

Measure Your Water

We have all heard the instruction: "Say when!" Well, if you add too much water to your soup, it will be runny, and flavorless.

But not adding enough water will render your soup ...well, not soup, and burnt. The same is true in life. As with any recipe, you must add enough water to balance your ingredients. Sometimes that balance comes later, when the soup is simmering. How do you know if it's going to work if you don't have everything you need? That's the beauty of your passion and purpose—you can add them in doses, pour them in all at once, or save them for when you might need them the most. Once you choose them, allow them to flow accordingly.

A well-thought-out recipe can help you get much further than by just guessing along the way. After all, some of the best soups are recipes passed down from generations, through family, and have been shared by people who love one another and celebrate their greatest moments. There is often something to be said for having a plan, a goal, or a purpose. However, you may be the kind of person who likes to experiment, and that is okay too.

Plan small goals, and each time you add another you will be one step closer to your dream. Maintain your momentum and continue cooking and believing in yourself. Planning out your goals is the key to success, as is dealing with problems along the way. Have purpose and the tenacity to adapt to unplanned changes. Have you ever tried a new recipe you thought you would love, and it turned out completely different from what you were expecting? Have you ever eaten something exquisite at a restaurant and wished you could have the recipe, only to find out there wasn't one? Perhaps you looked at two recipes for the exact same dish and were startled to find how much they varied. What role does the recipe play as you live your life, and why are they sometimes so easy and other times so mysterious or difficult?

If you are struggling with writing out your recipe, don't worry. As I mentioned, some people may prefer to exercise absolute creativity when making a new soup. You don't have to follow the exact recipe every step of the way. Cooking is not an exact science. It's fine if you have an idea for an ingredient but then decide it's not right for this soup. You can always make another soup with different ingredients in the future. If you step back and realize you are adding ingredients that do not seem to blend well, that's simply a sign that you need to refocus. Taste it. If it's not turning out well, look for something new to add or find a better ingredient. When planning the next stage of your soup, highlight actions that need more work, such as deciding whether to marinate your dish or thaw, chill, or soften it. Note what prep work is needed and what might be saved to add later during the cooking process. In the meantime, be resourceful and consider using unfamiliar or rare ingredients, and figure out where to locate them or how to find a good substitute.

Keep asking yourself if you are on the right track, because reflecting, reinventing, and constantly retasting your soup will ensure that you will keep your essence alive. Sometimes you may need to change the order of the ingredients, and when things get messy, clean them up and keep going. Adjust or make substitutions, *one at a time*, as you do not always know what a particular ingredient is doing in a recipe. If you make several substitutions at once and something goes wrong, it can be much more difficult to determine *which* element caused you to fail. Times will vary as they are mere guidelines, not rules. It's impossible to know exactly how long something will take before it's ready. Rely on your intuition and check your progress regularly. Never expect or assume.

You don't need to be a pro in your own life but looking inside yourself and adding a mentor may help you to understand the *ins* and *outs* and *whys*. Be educated and learn all you can. Knowledge can help you make better adjustments to your life at every stage. Learn from the people who have come before you and from your own failures. Don't always do things the same way. Try something different!

Together we are here to create your million-dollar soup. Remember, water is the base, and this is where it all begins. Once we have found our *purpose*, we can then begin to reflect on the other *ingredients* in our lives. They are all mutually exclusive and special, but they do interact with one another all the time. Your family is an *ingredient*. Friends are *ingredients*. Your career is an *ingredient*. Alone, they often carry very little *purpose* in your soup. They are one-notes. When assembled, however, they can become something quite magical. But they all need one common detail: the *water*. That's why we begin here. *Water*, the essence of life, is where this all begins. And throughout the rest of these chapters, we will continue to build on this fundamental and essential *soup/life base*.

CHAPTER 2

UNDERSTANDING FLAVORS:
DISCOVERING YOUR PURPOSE AND MISSION

Only the pure of heart can make good soup!

— Beethoven

While water will always act as the base for our million-dollar soup, it takes much more than water to create a tasty and fulfilling soup. It also requires understanding the role that different flavors play in each soup. Spices and other ingredients help distinguish one soup from another in the same way that we, as people, display distinguishing features and behaviors. What constitutes our *essence* makes each of us different and defines who we are as individuals. Each of us is made up of different ingredients, in the form of particular purposes, dreams, and objectives. So, each of us must take different steps in order to reach our goals.

When you are cooking, you always use your hands, your mind, and your creativity, in some form or another. In life it's the same. To achieve your goal, look at an imaginary roadmap to determine where you want to go and how to get there, to become the person you want to be. Clearly recognize and identify your destinations/goals and then create a life filled with purpose, grit, grace, and gratitude in order to arrive there.

Ask yourself who you are and what keeps you going. Identify your gifts, develop them, and share them with others. This is the path to achieving a meaningful life. Learn all you can about your dream/goal and thus become the *expert*. This will allow you to enhance the energy that surrounds you and to share it with others. When you do this, suddenly, your authenticity is revealed. You become your own master, having learned your craft, and you will be able to encourage others to follow their own dreams. It's just like a hearty soup on a cold winter's day, when all you need is the comfort of knowing that the soup is your energy, the driving force that keeps *you* engaged and provides value for *others* who wish to benefit from your expertise and presence.

When you fully understand what you want, the steps you need to take to pursue it will become apparent. They will be the flavors of your soup, the ingredients you will add to build these flavors. They can sometimes show up in a dream or just pop into your head while you are driving, taking a walk, or simply doing something you enjoy. If you want a million dollars or a million-dollar soup, start by asking yourself: What will this goal do for me? What will it feel like once I reach it? What steps should I take? If I want to help a million people learn to live their purpose, can I bring them together in a meaningful way?

Put all the ingredients into your pot, stir, and spread the flavors throughout. Understanding flavors will help you achieve your goal and build your soup. Consider, for example, that you want to open a local gym. To create a successful fitness facility, you need to target the right people (middle to upper class), retain good and knowledgeable trainers who look fit and who can implement systems. These are your flavors, right? If the gym, or the concept, is your water base, then the pieces within it are your carefully chosen flavors. You wouldn't hire incompetent trainers or staff who have no interest in fitness because that would definitely lead to failure. Identify exactly what you need and go after the best personnel. Some will simply show up out of the blue, and synchronicities will appear that indicate you are on the right path. It's about finding your tribe, your entourage, and the people who speak the same language as you do in their energy and actions. These are your foundation people, the people who mirror your expectations and goals. They will become some of your biggest cheerleaders. You can consider mentors in this group because they might add some magic ingredients that you didn't realize you needed.

Flavors represent your *action* steps; they are the ingredients for your million-dollar soup. You would not purchase shrimp and scallops to make a minestrone soup. However, you might do so if you are making a seafood chowder. What are your *action* steps? What sort of million-dollar soup are you making? Determine exactly what you want to achieve or create. If you want it to be great and give you lasting success, make sure it's your own idea, not something someone else wants. Be innovative, engage in discovery, and find something new to offer the world. Become the revolutionary or the leader in the kitchen who knows how to control the heat when the "goin' gets smokin'!" Choose a variety of flavors and remember, just as with a recipe, it will be easier to stay on track if you have a well-developed plan.

Most importantly, aim for a high goal. Go for the gusto, go for broke, pull out all the stops, and shoot the works. Les Brown, one of my favorite motivational speakers, says, "Most people fail in life, not because they aim too high and miss, but because they aim too low and hit." Many are content to be "a big fish in a small pond," instead of aiming for the ocean where they can really grow and spread their wings.

You must give yourself a chance to try that bigger platform, nurture your aspirations. By doing so, you will not only serve yourself but also give others the opportunity to live their best life and grow as large as they are meant to be. Sure, you may fail at first, but you never know until you try. If it doesn't go well, regroup, and try again. Just grab a new pot and start a different soup.

Untapped *potential* exists before, and after, every *failure*. *Failure* creates humility and helps you to gain clarity as you picture the next steps. *Failure* teaches you to see the full extent of what is possible. *Failure*, if nothing else, shows you how *not* to do something.

Never be so afraid of failure that you don't bother to try. I have failed so many times in my life, and I can say with the utmost certainty and confidence that each failure has taught me a life-changing lesson. Oh, I may not have felt that way at the time, but afterwards, I was clearly able to connect the dots and see a clearer picture of why that particular failure was necessary to my growth and later success. After all, I would rather fail at the big goals than succeed at the small ones. Aim for the moon, and, if you miss, you can live among the stars. Right? "Nothing ventured, nothing gained." So, what about you? Why not become a survivor of an *epic failure* in your moments of not hitting the mark?

Believe that *failure* is a bridge to the defining moment that will change your life. Being an epic failure means you flip the script on the story you tell yourself about the value of this failure. There are five tenets of being an epic failure:

1. You see failure as a catalyst for your own transformational growth because failure is our greatest teacher.

2. You value a life of being different by staying true to your own needs and desires.

3. You believe failure is a bridge to the defining moment that will change your life.

4. You use moments of failure to create a deeper awareness that you couldn't previously access.

5. Failure allows you to embrace a perpetual state of surrender and faith.

Have you ever been in a make-or-break situation in which every part of you knew that you wanted to say *yes* but everything around you was saying *no*? You knew that you had to act … immediately!

Here is a story that will drive home those points and will show that sometimes we just need to make decisions based on a strong belief in ourselves and go for it!

In my early forties, I started a business, a kick-butt fitness gym. I thought it out, I did my research, I had a plan, and everything about me was like *YES*! Let's start this business! Let's do it! I signed a lease on a space, I had all the equipment, and I followed all the steps to hit the ground running...

Have you ever actually tried to hit the ground running? It's like jumping from a moving vehicle! That's what happened to me. Shortly before I was to launch, I shattered my ankle—like totally obliterated it—and suddenly everything around me was saying, "Don't do it, don't do it, don't do it!" Was this a sign from the universe? It couldn't be! And besides, the decision had been made, the lease was signed, the ink was dry. I had committed to it.

Then I remembered a quote from another inspirational figure and spiritual leader, Bishop T.D. Jakes, whose words never cease to excite me. On one of his awesome videos on 'YouTube', he says: "Do it broke, do it scared, do it trembling, do it on crutches, do it from a wheelchair, just do it! You don't want to end up in a nursing home, sitting on a bedpan, wondering what would have happened, if you'd had more courage. You don't want your dying thought to be, "I wish I had...". One thing you will never find is more time. You have the key! Unlock the door and step into your destiny!"

I *had* to follow my gut. I *had* to forget about the *back* button. You can't just *ctrl+alt+delete* in life. I had to ignore all escape routes and force myself to power through. I knew I couldn't take back all the decisions I had already made. I realized that, although I literally wasn't able to walk, there was much more to it than that. I had started the ball rolling, and I couldn't just stop it. Think about the decisions you make in your life—getting married, building a house, taking that job, really pushing yourself out of your comfort zone. It's scary. Really scary! But who would we be if we didn't do it? If we kept walking over that well-worn *easy path*, it's likely we wouldn't be who we are today!

That's where belief and faith come in. It's scary and uncomfortable, and sometimes we fail, but we have to go for it. It takes believing in ourselves first. So that's what I did. I looked at myself and thought, "Okay, J.L., you are going to have people coming into your gym, looking for help and guidance. You might not be able to show them all the exercises or lead in the way that you usually do, but your attitude isn't broken. Nor is your outlook on life or your spirit. You can *still* offer all of that to everyone who comes through the door."

I set my sights on customer service, greeting everyone with a huge smile and a big, loud *welcome*. I treated everyone with respect and dignity and gave everyone a personal experience to boost them through every session and keep them coming back again and again. Because even before the injury, I believed that, if I could keep being my *best* person and help others do the same, I would have succeeded. I also inspired, motivated, and shared my knowledge with others and hired four trainers who became my core group and part of my gym family.

And after all of that, my fitness business was an amazing success, and I was asked to speak in front of a few thousand people within the franchise to inspire other owners. And *that* is when things got really interesting, and the most amazing thing happened! Unbeknownst to me, in the audience that day was my biggest hero, the legendary Les Brown (I quoted him earlier) and he heard *me* speak. Afterwards, he looked at me and in his booming voice said, "Young lady, you should be speaking for a living!" Wow!

And then, over the next few days, more people cornered me in the elevator, in the ladies' room—and a few even chased me down the street! They wanted to thank me for inspiring them. I had touched something in them. I thought: "Look at all the people I impacted. Maybe I should be speaking for a living." Well, it was then I realized that I wanted more. So, I started moving forward to position myself as a speaker, and that is another thing I'm passionate about and pursuing today. A whole new purpose was revealed, simply by listening to my gut!

Discovery—the Spell Behind Your Million-Dollar Soup

The value of what you are doing is not the goal per se, but rather, it's to be the person you want to become, or the soup you want to make, while pursuing your *purpose*. The steps you take, the rewards you gain, and the *failures* you inevitably learn from are the things that mold you into becoming the *best version of yourself*. The soup gets better and better. And this is what *really matters* because inevitably, the soup is who you want to be. As others taste it, they will want more. They will want to make a soup of their own, once they *feel inspired* after tasting yours.

This is your chance to create anything you want in life. It begins with an awareness, then a lot of thinking, and finally a decision to commit to making that million-dollar soup. You've got to be hungry, meaning you need to want to get the most out of your life. Get out there and *DISCOVER!* Be an adventurer, and keep going the extra mile, just like the head chef in the kitchen who has all his systems in place for synchronicity with his team and, most of all, within himself. *Discovery* helps to create *balance* and give you hope that you are on to bigger and brighter horizons. I can't tell you how many times I have taken risks through finding a part of myself I didn't even know existed. Becoming an explorer gives you the *passion* to always evolve because there is always something new and fresh in front of you.

Passion is everything in life. The value is that you achieve a better life and become a better person along the way. It satiates different aspects of who you are: self-respect and self-love, confidence, joy, and a true appreciation for life. You become the best version of you. Like tasting an amazing soup, it's a sublime experience to find your *passion* and *purpose*. But that's the whole point; it just becomes more and more satisfying and rewarding as you add more *flavor* and more *ingredients* to it. There is no better feeling than recognizing the direction in which your life is heading. Nobody knows the *how*, but all can resonate with the *delight* of the journey. You are able to live on your own terms and have the opportunity to lead others, leave your mark, and make the world a better place because you were here. You can have anything you want, and there is so much wonder and so many incredible places to see and things to experience. You may find financial success and a healthy mind, body, and spirit to appreciate the things and the people around you. You will also be able to better other people's lives, which is the biggest gift you can give yourself and the world.

Maneuvering Flavors

Choose the best flavors for you. By that I mean we all must engage in a journey that supports our individual *passion*. To start, write down your goals and the whys and wants that support them. What will they do for you? Help more people? Generate more time? Release you to freedom? Enhance your health? Put all your wants together to identify ingredients and flavors. The best outcome will emerge, once you have stripped your thoughts down to the essential parts of who you are and who you want to be.

Don't hold back. You truly can do or be anything. I'm turning fifty soon. I've been checking off my list of wants for years. I've jumped out of planes, learned to scuba dive, swum with sharks, traveled a decent amount, raised my children, started two fitness clubs, and watched them succeed. I have helped others, written a few books, performed classical piano pieces, and spoken on stage in front of hundreds and thousands of people. And now I want to do even more. The next thing on my to-do list is to run the Boston Marathon.

More than anything though, I want to inspire millions of people with my million-dollar soup! These are my *flavors*, the *goals* that keep me purpose-driven and passionate. You need to choose your path! Go down it and stay on it and never turn around! Think about the dreams you had as a child and the activities that you have a natural talent for. And again, make sure that your purpose is driven by your own passions and not by someone else's. More often than not, we can become very comfortable living someone else's dream and thereby lose sight of the fact that we have given up on ourselves.

Finding Your Own Mission

Now that you understand the versatile and important role that choosing your flavors plays in creating a purposeful life, I want to help you find your own version of *purpose* and *engagement*. We should all, as humans, hold on to something that truly motivates us and resonates with us. The more passion-driven your pursuits are, the better they are. *Don't* spread yourself too thin but *do* fall in love with many things. Don't become a hamster on a wheel. Come out of the box, stretch, relax, breathe, and engage in breakthroughs for yourself and your community. Don't be the can of congealed, gelatinous soup. Keep making your *very own*!

In searching for your *passion*, you must first find your *platform*. What do you like? What do you love to do? What is your gift? What did you dream about becoming as a child? You need to find your pot and your base. Write them down, discover what you're good at, believe in yourself, plan, and consider what you want to get out of this life. To be a mother? What is her million-dollar soup? What will she need to make the best soup? Patience, empathy, nurturing instincts, and so forth. She can share what she has inside of herself. How can she add *value* to others and to the world around her? How can she make a difference? These are the questions a new mother might be asking herself along the way.

As for you, what will spring you out of bed in the morning with excitement? Preparing for big goals can change the course of your entire life. Waking up in the morning can be the most exciting part of your day. Thinking about your dreams can set the tone for your day. Dreams can motivate, inspire, and help you to achieve any goal. I promise that you will never feel the need to hit the snooze button again if you keep your dreams at the forefront of your mind.

There will be no ambition to chase without dreams, no incentive to reach for the brass ring. It's impossible to achieve anything in life without *goals*, and we need to have a *dream* to set and, ultimately, pursue our *goals*. Spend time dreaming, let your mind run wild, and consider where your life is headed. If you are not actively setting *goals* that are moving in the direction of your *dreams*, then perhaps there is no better time than now to start *dreaming* once again. *Dreams* are one of the most important *flavors* in your soup. They take on so much and truly come through in the end. Once you start to *dream* big, your original base of just water will begin to turn into something else, a special and flavorful *catalyst* that becomes the *aura* of *energy* that you invite around you.

Another step toward mining your passion is to think about your role models. They may be real people or perhaps even a character in a book, film, or movie. Are they doing or have they done something that speaks to you? You can follow them, meet them, and get in touch, or you can let them motivate and inspire you. Watch inspiring movies and read motivational books and biographies that interest and excite you. In doing so, you will find that you begin to connect with the authors' or characters' energy, and something special will start to simmer.

I recall watching the movie 'The Pianist' back in the early 2000s. All it took was one part of the movie, close to the end, when the main character played an incredible piece on the piano. I replayed it once and decided in that moment to return to my music.

When I was younger, I loved playing piano, and I became quite good at it. Something happened during that time that led to me quit playing altogether. But all it took was one movie to inspire me to sit right back onto the deep rich brown piano bench in front of the Heinzman Baby Grand I'd grown up playing. I played and played until the tendons and muscles in my hands, arms, shoulders, and neck were screaming.

In 2002, after a lengthy hiatus from my music, I enrolled in a piano competition. I was to perform a difficult piece of music by Beethoven. I knew this sixteen-page piece of music like the back of my hand. I was so ready for it and even decided to bring my mother along to surprise her. We had been estranged for years, and we were finally reconciling as she battled cancer, so I thought it could be part of our process of reconnecting. She had no idea that I had come back to playing and performing after so long away from it. I really wanted to wow her. So, the pressure was on!

The lights were warm on my face. I sat down at the piano and began playing. My fingers moved fast, but not effortlessly; they felt like they were in mud. As my fingers moved through the notes, I found myself repeating the same part over and over. I was unable to move past it because I couldn't remember what came next. I couldn't just stop playing, so I kept returning to that familiar part of the piece. I re-played it several times.

My mind kept racing with how I could get myself out of the memory lapse, while listening to an inner monologue of: "How many more times can I repeat these same measures before people notice? The judges have surely caught on by now and some of the other pianists probably have too." I knew for sure that my mother, who had been a piano teacher for more than thirty-five years, had noticed. Well, eventually I just decided that I would remember. I relaxed my shoulders and willed those notes back into my fingers. Muscle memory came over me, and I was able to work through the piece and finish it off.

The adjudicator knew I was having trouble remembering the transitional element of the piece, and as he approached the stage to speak after my performance, my heart was in my throat. I was sure he would have some sort of chiding comment or negative review. He grabbed the mic, and I will never forget what he said: "Today we had a rare opportunity to witness a person who doesn't quit!"

Can you believe it? No criticism, just genuine praise for making it through a tough piece. I went on to take first place in the competition that day, and I was beyond ecstatic. But nothing was more rewarding than having my mother stand up, pull her wig off (she had lost all her hair from chemo), and wave it around from her seat in the audience, as she screamed as loudly as her soft, breathy voice, affected by radiation treatments, would allow: "That's my girl!" Can you say: "my cup runneth over?" This event was even more amazing because my mother, a normally very quiet, prim, and proper sort who always acted like quite the lady, proudly walked toward the front of the concert hall and embraced me, something she rarely did. I will never forget her beautiful, pale-blue eyes as they sparkled with tears as she cried and praised my performance. Her tears acted as an elixir for our relationship as it took on a whole new level that day.

As you follow your *dreams* and *passion*, you nourish your *soul*. This opens the doors to self-discovery and finding something that is uniquely yours. The problem for many people is that they don't take the time to think. Thinking is essential in order to brew, stew, and fundamentally come to terms with what we love and manifest what we want before making our soup. Wake up and always remember that you can stop where you are right now and shift into something completely different. People are constantly putting *ingredients* together, but they haven't even decided to make *soup* yet. That's because they don't know what they want.

We all have a million-dollar *soup* inside of us, but we may be running around with a pot filled with just *water*. We haven't put anything into it, haven't even turned on the stove. We are ignoring the kitchen. Every day the opportunity to make our million-dollar soup slips away. We are coasting through life, collecting dust. But the purpose is always there if we decide to see it. Does this resonate with you? Are you thinking maybe it's too late for you? Well, no, it's not. You can do it whenever you want. Some people have already started their soup, and they don't realize it or don't have the wherewithal to finish it. Don't waste your chance to live the life you have always dreamed of. Make your million-dollar soup here and now!

If you have gotten this far, then you have already filled the pot with your *base*. Armed with a pot full of *water*, the sky is the limit. In this chapter we demonstrated how the *ingredients*, and their resulting flavors are indicative of your *passion*. *Flavors* combine and collaborate in soup to form a delicious melange. In true synergistic form, "the sum is always greater than its parts." The same is true in life. Your *flavors* are your *passions*—the *longings* that get you up in the morning and leave you feeling excited for the day to come, and fulfilled, once you complete them.

Just as you can pick and choose your most favorable *ingredients* from a fresh garden, the same goes for *people*. Select from those who truly leave you feeling energized and fulfilled. Mix and match; don't settle for just one. Enjoy them and go back for seconds. Perhaps Oprah said it best: "*Passion* is energy. Feel the *power* that comes from focusing on what excites you."

CHAPTER 3

EVALUATING YOUR MEASUREMENTS:
CREATING BALANCE IN YOUR LIFE

> *Happiness is not a matter of intensity but of balance and order and rhythm and harmony.*
>
> — Thomas Merton

As in cooking, *balance* is a crucial part of having a meaningful, happy life. It's where *perfection* lives... a destination where there is *just enough* to make it *perfect*. In one way or another, we are all on a crucial journey to establish and capture *balance*. But as easy as it may sound, or as clear as the concept may be, we often feel like we are chasing something unattainable. It's elusive at best, very difficult to find at worst. Life tosses and turns us around to the extent that even the most focused and dedicated of us fall well short of creating *balance*. In all aspects of our life, *balance* is of utmost importance to all of us.

Creating a wonderful, well-balanced soup comes down to a careful, thoughtful process of initial measurements, regular adjustments, and consistent stability in the details. Accurate *measuring* is essential to adding or taking away in your life. Finding *balance* within your soul means that you have found a rhythm that makes you feel secure, because this is what you were born to feel and do. Live your purpose with proper *balance* and *measure*.

Everything in life is about finding a happy balance... between light and dark, good and bad, serious and funny, happy and sad, sweet and sour. Too much of one thing is just as damaging as too little. We all love light, but we only know light because of darkness. It's important to be happy, but sometimes experiencing sadness offers us a measure of perspective we might not otherwise have. It's wonderful to joke around, but, at pivotal times, you must maintain a level of seriousness because your dream is not going to fall into your lap. You will have to experience the ups and downs and face some of your fears to create your own transformation. Moving from darkness into the light is like taking a deep breath and enjoying the freshness and freedom.

You must determine what is right for you. No one else can do this. Weigh and consider everything you add or subtract in your life. Of course, there are ways to decide what *measurement* is right for you, just as when you are making soup. The simple act of *measuring* often leads you toward finding *balance*. Stick your spoon in and taste it, or in life, jump in and experience it. Balance is achieved through your experiences—a little bit of this and a little bit of that, until you have it just right.

It's easy to measure things in the kitchen... a cup of this, a tablespoon of that, a pinch of something else, but it's not necessarily so in life where you can't just add a standard amount and expect the perfect balance of flavors. For example, if you aim to be fit, you can't just work out like a maniac every day and expect to thrive. You need to recuperate by supplementing your workouts with recovery, as well as a healthy diet and plenty of rest. It takes time, so don't expect change in just the first week alone. Transformation is a never-ending process, and you will find that, as you begin to flow with your soup, you will receive signals indicating when shift and change are needed.

First determine what results you want, just as with cooking. After choosing what you want to cook, it's time to measure your ingredients and make important decisions about what to use or not to use. The same is true in almost every lifetime endeavor that you pursue. Consider your desire to become a good salesperson. You may study several salespeople and discover which techniques work for you, and then you measure how many of those to use. These are the action steps that lead you to achieving your goals. Of course, this is no easy process. There are many factors involved and a lot of ingredients to consider and measure.

With cooking, as in life, you may not always have the exact measurements you need for that perfect recipe. In fact, these ingredients will sometimes change, depending on how you are feeling. Spicy? Not spicy? You can decide. Taste it and see. One day you may feel like a cream soup. Another day you may want a consommé. The lovely thing that cooking and life have in common is that you can't really go wrong. You can always adjust along the way. Taste your soup or try out your new job/activity and see if it works for you. No problem if it doesn't. Simply change it. Never, ever be afraid of change, especially if you want to discover more. Remember that *discovery* is a key *ingredient* to maybe finding the next amazing *recipe* or your next greatest *idea*.

Cooking may sometimes require precise measurements, and using the right combination of ingredients, time, energy, and temperature is necessary to create exactly what is desired. Estimating or assessing the extent, quality, value, or effect of your goals will help you determine how much or how little time, energy, money, or education to add to your soup. Constantly monitor your life so that you can be sure you are on the right track. Never, ever leave a boiling pot of soup unattended. Doing so can potentially create very negative results, burning it, or changing the flavor altogether, after which you will need to start all over again. Keep an eye on what you are adding or subtracting all the time. Remember, you are the head chef of the kitchen, and you always have to be in control.

Measuring creates *balance* which, in turn, creates enjoyment. A well-balanced, satisfying soup results from good ingredients, time, and tasting. The same is true in life. In your soup, you may want potatoes, cream, cheese, and some chicken broth, while in life you may choose fitness, relationships, parenthood, and a career. Choosing what you want in your life will allow you to set realistic goals for triumphant achievements. You are the architect of your life—it's time to start designing. Also know that you can change the ingredients at any time as you delve into self-discovery. Creating boundless options for experimenting will only lead to an energetic and resilient life.

Balance from the Beginning

Over our evolution as humans, we have recognized *balance* as an essential component to a happy life. This concept plays out in many arenas of life. While cooking, have you ever noticed that many excellent meals have a contrast of soft and crunchy?

Consider *nachos*—crispy tortilla chips, gooey cheese, creamy guacamole, crunchy lettuce, maybe some soft and juicy tomatoes. It's a symphony of contrast that creates *balance*. Or it could be a creamy and chunky dish, like clam chowder, or even a salty and sweet dish, like salmon and cream cheese.

In each of these dishes, often the contrasts in the measurements and ingredients create the balance that is so joyous to our palates. Opposites often complement each other, just as they do in everyday life. A wise countrywoman once said: "You can't have a rainbow without a little rain." A beautiful sunny day can't be appreciated without knowing what a dark, rainy day feels like. And you will better appreciate true happiness, when you know how true suffering feels.

As you can see, balance is vitally important. Let me be clear, though. Balance doesn't mean a one-to-one ratio. You would never put in one cup of sugar and one cup of salt. A teaspoon here, a pinch there creates balance. Balance is a big-picture concept, an overall view. Would you balance your life by spending the same amount of time at a bar as you would with your family, or an equal amount of time at a gym as you would at your work? Having well-balanced measurements creates order in your life. In cooking, with a bit more of this and less of that, you will establish the sweet and salty balance and taste that pleases the palate. In life, making proper time for family and for business creates a nice, rewarding balance in your life. Know your priorities as well and when to stop and take some time for yourself.

Consider all aspects of your life when you are striving for balance—your relationships, health, business/work, as well as your emotional well-being. It's too easy to get off balance, especially if you really enjoy your work or have a lot invested, as is the case when you run your own business. Growing a business from scratch is like raising a child. You invest so much care, thought, and time into it, and it's easy to feel consumed with the everyday tasks. In that scenario, you might not be able to find proper balance, knowing far too well that you have no choice but to give a great deal of your time and attention to this new endeavor. Eventually things will even out. But for now, you are going to have to sacrifice some element of balance for the betterment of your goals and dreams.

Losing Balance

In many ways, the opposite of balance is not imbalance. In fact, it can be *chaos*. Having too much or too little of one thing, either too sweet or salty, too much work or not enough, not enough time for some things or too much time for others, may easily lead to chaos. If you disrupt the taste or goal, you may experience stress and anxiety, and ultimately end up in overall failure and, oftentimes, complete chaos. Establishing and maintaining balance in your life will help you avoid disruptive chaos.

I entered a state of chaos when, after opening one successful gym, I decided it was time to open another. At the time, I thought it was the logical next step so, after doing all the research, I opened my second club and, before long, both were running smoothly. That is, until they weren't. This marked the beginning of an exhausting roller coaster ride that I didn't know how to stop.

I always understood on a deep level that all big things developed from something small. The seed of every habit is a single, tiny decision. Simply repeat and expand on it and it will grow stronger. Building a great habit is like cultivating a delicate rose; it needs to be done one day at a time. The problem that developed with my gym was that I couldn't seem to find the *balance* to maintain two gyms, two sets of employees, two sets of equipment, all in two separate locations! Two, two, two! If only I could have cloned another me! It was overwhelming. I would nurture one until all was fine, and the other would begin to fail in spectacular fashion. Then I would take more care with the other and the first would start to flounder. I was sometimes driving thirty-five miles up to six times a day, back and forth between these two gyms! What I needed was a system.

Prevailing wisdom suggests that the best way to be successful is to set goals and follow specific steps until said goals are reached. But that doesn't always work. In my case, I was lacking a *system*. Instead of concerning myself with achieving an elusive result, which was to be profitable in both locations without making myself sick, I should have been developing a clearly defined set of processes that could have led to the result I wanted. In other words, a *system*. Putting *systems* in place lead to success. So that's exactly what I did, and it worked phenomenally well.

When your soup, just as with your life, is out of *balance*, it's easy to taste/feel that something is not right. If you inadvertently add too much of an *ingredient*, you may easily sabotage the whole essence of your soup. But do you know what? It's just as easy to add some other ingredient that you haven't tried before. Step back, assess, discover, re-evaluate, and work toward restoring a *balance*. If you don't take measures to re-create yourself, and you stay stuck in a rut, people around you will notice that you're off-balance. When you're leading an unbalanced life, you will wear your despair on your sleeve. The discomfort of your chaos will be obvious. You are now lost, unhinged, and are finding it difficult to resume your once steady life.

But you certainly aren't alone; we have all been there! You may need to start over. If you have the right mindset, you will likely find yourself in a position where you can adjust and grow. You can learn from your mistakes and begin again. Or you may associate chaos and bad feelings with what you were doing at the time and then become fearful of doing it again. First, know where you are going. To be out of *balance* with regard to going after your goal means you are either not doing enough, or you are doing too much. That's why *measuring* helps. Be open to mistakes and starting over. Imagine if Edison, the Wright brothers, Walt Disney, and others had not continued to believe until they achieved!

If you feel that you don't have a good worktime/free-time *balance*, on your next day off, consider some new ways to spend your free time in an effort to *balance* it out with the work time that you have been putting in. If certain people are causing the *imbalance*, find a better way of dealing with them, or simply decide to let them go.

What is the first step? Recognize that your results are falling short of where you would like them to be. This requires a sober assessment of your life. Sometimes it hurts to admit your faults and shortcomings. But this is okay. Forgiveness begins with yourself. Don't beat yourself up. Acknowledge the mistakes, forgive yourself, forgive others, and move on. Don't stay stuck or congealed like that canned soup. You have come too far with your fresh *ingredients* to go back to shoving yourself into a can. It's extremely dark and lonely in there and a very stunted environment for growth and transformation to take place. As Les Brown says, "...You can't read the label if you are stuck in the can."

This reminds me of another story about my *epic failures*. When I think about my life path and my failures, especially when it comes to recognizing my mistakes, my first triathlon springs to mind.

Leading up to my first triathlon, I was training in a way that felt best for me, often ignoring other athletes' advice. I have always liked doing things my way. After all, that's part of my *epic failure* credo: "You value a life of being different by staying true to your own needs and desires." There were times when I didn't follow the standard advice and, consequently, I failed miserably. Until one day, when I figured it out!

I had been training and practicing for months, visualizing my success while making every muscle in my body sore in preparation, but when race day came along it quickly became obvious that my methods had not set me up for success, but rather for failure.

Most triathlons start off with everyone huddled together at the starting line, and then everyone dives into the water for that first leg of the race, the swimming part. It's chaotic and invigorating, as all of the swimmers' jostle for a spot to get into their rhythm. Everyone starts the race with the front crawl. I didn't. I had practiced with the breaststroke (I know, please get a good hearty laugh out of this one if you are a swimmer, at my expense, I beg of you, as I assure you, I am laughing too!) and planned to use it in the race, since it was my most comfortable stroke and I thought that I would be fine with it. Well, I wasn't, and I soon discovered why. The front crawl is the most efficient stroke and the movements of it require the least amount of space to be effective, making it the logical choice for when you need to break away from a pack at the beginning of a triathlon.

Imagine being in a crowd of people where everyone is doing one thing and you are trying to do another. You are going to be about as popular as garlic bread at Dracula's wedding reception. And this was compounded by the fact that I had a quick sprint off the start, so I was able to snag a brief lead, only to then be overrun by the other competitors, as they torpedoed past me with their more efficient front crawl. I eventually fell very far behind, and I was both embarrassed but relieved to imagine that soon I would be languishing in last place. You can imagine that this would be a bit of a relief, since there was no one else around me to interfere with my huge strokes, but the one piece of advice I had decided to follow, that also turned out to be a big mistake, was to wear a wetsuit. Although it did keep me warm, it made my strokes so much more awkward that, even if I had the whole lake to myself, it would still be difficult. I have always been an athlete, but in that moment, I felt very much like a fish out of water. I realized I was in way over my head. But, as always, I ploughed through.

When I finally reached the second part of the triathlon, the bicycling, I hopped on my bike with excitement, and while feeling very embarrassed about my performance in the water, I was also kind to myself and kept right on trying. I knew how fast I could ride and knew that the best was still yet to come and that I could still make it happen. Forward ever, backward never. This had been a lifelong dream! I kept focused on the black numbers on the legs in front of me, which is where our bib number is written once we register at the beginning of the race. A smile spread slowly but surely as one by one I passed one biker after another until the numbers became clusters of unending numbers. I chanted, "just one more...just one more... just more more!" as my bike and I overtook as many riders as was possible.

Next up, was the transition to the last leg of the triathlon, the run and I jumped off my bike and started running. I continued the same way, passing one competitor after another. And when I finally felt the excitement exploding around me while loved ones and friends gathered along the sidelines to encourage and blow horns and encourage everyone, the hair on the back of my neck raised and I could remember every race I'd ever been in since I'd been a small child. I was born to compete and even though I couldn't feel my legs, I pumped my arms and ran with everything I had left, and smiled and sprinted in, passing and surprising a great many competitors to the delight of my family who had been at the finish line. Wow!!!! I will never forget this day!!

I ended up feeling like the biggest winner. I certainly didn't do as well as I had hoped, but, in the same breath, which I was gradually catching, I was feeling proud that I hadn't given up. The long road of becoming a triathlete was still ahead of me, and despite being in last place during the swimming portion, I let go of my failure right then and there and just kept pushing myself to see how far I could go and to see what I could do in that moment with what I had inside of me. I was so proud of myself, and I learned so much about life that day.

The humility I felt after the triathlon was palpable. And the learning I gained through it helped me to develop a new understanding of how triathletes need to compete. And that acknowledgment helped me become a much better competitor. So, you see, failure can turn people into champions.

Trying harder is not always the answer to achieving more. It doesn't offer any real promise of achievement and can often destroy your chances for success. You must learn *how* to try repeatedly in order to have a fighting chance.

So, was I going to try harder for my next triathlon? Not really, I had already tried pretty hard but I didn't place last. Instead, I sought out one of the greatest triathlon coaches around, a real find, someone who'd been a Canadian triathlete himself and began to work with him to learn how I can do better. We met every morning at 5:30 AM before I went to work (this with three daughters, a one-eyed dog named Mandy, and a travelling husband). At one point after a couple of weeks of training, I asked him how I was doing. I pleaded with him to be honest, and he told me that I was one of the worst swimmers that he had ever coached. Yikes! But guess what? I kept coming back, and my improvement over the next few weeks shocked us both because we were seeing how much I had improved in all three areas of the triathlon, especially my swimming. I learned how to become a more successful competitor. I have now completed six triathlons, and I'm currently aiming my sights on a half or full Iron Man competition as well as the Boston Marathon.

So here is the next step: Let yourself out of the can. Learn how to do better. You can do this through reading books like this one and so many others. If you know how to do better, the chances are you will achieve it. Think of young children making a dessert. They use flour, water, and some sugar. To them, these ingredients are like the nectar of the gods, but as they LEARN more, they discover that they can continue to improve. I remember many crazy recipes my three daughters created when they were young. I had to swallow some of their creations without hurting their feelings, though sometimes I secretly spat out some of it, careful to avoid getting caught. Now that they are grown, their concoctions have become incredible morsels of delight. I'm so glad I swallowed and took one for the team. It was worth it!

Awareness and understanding about what you need to do to improve yourself and become what you want to be is essential for growth. Ask yourself whether or not you have been following the steps. If not, why not? How can you change this? Are your goals unbalanced? Maintaining balance is a way of life, and if you feel unbalanced, it's because you have done something that is not in line with your goals. You have taken a wrong turn or are rushing things by not taking the time and effort it requires.

If your soup is unbalanced, then it may be as easy as adding in some cream, a squeeze of citrus, a dash of salt, or just about anything else to rebalance the flavor. The same is true in life. If you are working too much and not getting anywhere, you may just need to change something up. Perhaps you need a quick weekend getaway. If you gained ten pounds during the holidays, why not focus on your diet and return to the gym? The beauty of balance is that, when it's *off*, it can still be within your grasp. Simply soldier on and keep trying to capture it in your life, just as in your soup.

Gauging and Then Creating Your Balance

How do you know if you are out of balance? Sometimes it will be so obvious that you just can't miss it. However, at other times it's not so evident. Perhaps a disagreement with your significant other has stayed with you. Unsure why, you continue along your path, but you know something is wrong. Gradually the discomfort becomes something much greater, and then you feel off balance. You still think nothing of it. But as the conflict rises and your soup thickens, it starts to cloud your days. What started as a small disagreement has now become a much greater problem. What started as unsteadiness has you now totally unbalanced. Don't fret. You're not trapped. You can stop the feeling from washing over you.

Like the chef in charge of his kitchen taking control of the whole restaurant, *you* are the person who must take control of your life. Don't be discouraged, even if your soup bubbles over. Again, step back, turn the heat down, control the environment, and measure your new course of action. Regrouping is such an important step to remaining balanced. This might sound like opposite forces, but it's like the philosophy of yin and yang that helps us learn from the chaos and create new discoveries by exploring new measurements.

Balance is variable. It comes in many shapes and sizes. But, as I tell people, you know the difference between balance and chaos when you feel them. For many, the results of any endeavor are a good indicator of whether you are in balance. A successful career but a disastrous home life indicates that things are not properly balanced. Conversely, a rich home life and a terrible career may also indicate that you are lacking balance. If you are to succeed in your life, then constantly be on the lookout to gauge your balance. In doing so you are gifted with an amazing opportunity to change the recipe, to add or subtract ingredients. Instead of pouring some exercise or social time or your career into a measuring cup, you are using your feelings to measure when the cup within your mind is full. Only you can do this, because it's specific to you and your needs.

Recognizing and setting the pathway toward achieving the little goals is often the greatest way to measure your balance and open the way toward the bigger ones. Accomplishments are gained by using tools to keep you striving and moving forward. Tools are the means by which you can achieve your goals. Once you accomplish one goal, you can set yourself a new goal by using another tool. For example, when you learn something and become better, you can use this tool to improve your abilities. In addition, the example you leave for others may serve as a tool to help them achieve their own goals. Confidence is a tool. Persistence and discipline are tools. Our happiness, as well as the happiness of those around us, can also be a tool to measure our lives. If the people around us are miserable, we should all revisit how we are living.

We should ask ourselves questions such as:

1. Does this relationship serve me?
2. Does this career serve me?
3. Do the friends I spend time with make me happy?

Additionally, consider these three elements in life you need to succeed:

1. Things to make you *money*
2. Things to make you *happy*
3. Things to make you *better*

Consider people around you, jobs, places, activities, and belongings. If they don't accomplish one of those three accomplishments for you, simply take them out of the equation. Only then can you start measuring the correct amounts of the ingredients that are there for your use to re-create balance. You can consider other aspects of living that might otherwise help you secure balance.

Here are a few:

1. Rest
2. Discovery
3. Learning
4. Exercise
5. Curiosity
6. Self-analysis

To create balance, first assess your life as it is right now. Then make informed decisions about setting and sustaining goals and you will see the difference that balance makes in promoting growth. Along the way, you may wish to take some calculated risks, as you believe in yourself and others, thinking that anything is possible while you await the anticipated outcome.

In life, we need to have faith and believe that we can achieve what we set our sights on. You don't need to know how right at the onset. The way will reveal itself. Demonstrate self-confidence, assess your life, and make a conscious decision to become balanced by accepting necessary change. Set realistic goals, take calculated risks, and become adept at reassessing yourself. Try your best to remain positive and find the lesson in everything, even when the learning process seems dark and unclear. Remember, there is always a way from the darkness into the light. Just lift the cover and let the steam of your soup show you the way.

CHAPTER 4

A DASH OF SALT:
RECOGNIZING ADVERSITY WITH A GRAIN OF SALT

The cure for anything is salt water: sweat, tears, or the sea.

– Karen Blixen

Seasoning enhances the taste of food by bringing out its natural flavors. *Community* acts in the same way. When *community* flavors are in alignment, we bring out one another's distinct strengths. This amounts to pure heart-centered *collaboration*.

With any kind of cooking, you have most likely doused a rather heavy load of *salt* on top. *Salt* enhances flavor but, as with anything, it should be used in moderation. Too much salt spoils the taste and too little may leave a bland taste. However, every palate is different. There is no accounting for taste at any level. Everyone has individual tastes that require a different amount of salt. Salt can act in contrasting ways - by turning up the volume of already salty flavors or dialing down a bitter taste. I particularly enjoy using salt to balance sweet and salty tastes, such as in a dark-chocolate, sea-salt bar. Mmm!

And the variety of ways we can use *salt* when we cook doesn't stop at *seasoning*. *Salt* is also an effective preservative. In fact, salt is one of the first preservatives ever used. Although the need has decreased considerably over the years because of refrigeration, salt, or sodium, still plays a big role in reducing the growth of pathogens and organisms that can spoil our food.

The truth is that you simply can't prepare a tasty, enjoyable meal without at least using a little salt. It's literally a chef's best friend and a staple in every single kitchen across the world. It crosses geography, national origin, socioeconomic conditions, background, and history. Everyone, no matter who you are or where you come from, has tasted salt. And just like most things in life, there are a variety of salts.[1]

Here is a taste of how salt's many varieties can be used as a metaphor for life:

1. Table Salt: Also known as "iodized salt," table salt has very fine grains and contains potassium iodide and an anticaking agent that helps prevent it from clumping. This salt is good to keep away people who want to stick to you just for the ride. Get rid of them; nobody wants to work in a clump.

2. Kosher Salt: If you have room for only one salt in your pantry, opt for kosher salt. Its texture is light but coarse

---

[1] https://www.countryliving.com/food-drinks/g30689559/salt-types/

(which helps you avoid oversalting) and it dissolves easily. We all must learn to be "light," and in this, we are almost ethereal and can give our problems to the vortex, which helps to dissolve obstacles.

3. Himalayan Pink Salt: The purest of all salt, Himalayan pink salt is harvested from the Khewra Salt Mine in the Himalayan mountains of Pakistan. Its beauty and grace are so majestic that cooking with it makes you feel like a shaman. The pristine element and its pink beauty remind us to be pure and to illuminate our auras with a pink sheen.

4. Sea Salt: Harvested from evaporated seawater, the taste of sea salt can be either very heavy or light, depending on where it's harvested, so taste it first. Don't ever overdo anything and remember that tempering yourself with new experiences might require you to test out the waters before you take a huge chunk out of the unknown.

5. Celtic Grey Sea Salt: Harvested from Atlantic tidal ponds off the coast of France, Celtic Sea salt is also known as *sel gris* (French for "gray salt"). This salt is exotic and has a peppery taste. Be different in your life; recreate yourself while remaining pure.

6. Fleur De Sel: Like Celtic Sea salt, *fleur de sel* (French for "flower of salt") is harvested from evaporated seawater, but it comes specifically from the coast of Brittany. This salt is often described as smelling like, and tasting of, the sea. Think of how you can use our metaphor of water as the base for our lives. Flower salt reminds us that we are limitless and vast beings, just like the ocean.

7. Flake Salt: Like *sel gris* and *fleur de sel*, flake salt is harvested from evaporated seawater, although its shape and texture are quite different. We are all built from the same material, but each of us has a different shape and texture. Flake salt reminds us that we are all unique and beautiful.

8. Red Hawaiian Salt: Red Hawaiian salt is sea salt mixed with iron-oxide-rich volcanic clay. Its flavor is described as nutty. Yes! We all get nutty sometimes, but that's okay. It's a reminder that we are human and have the power to evolve.

9. Black Hawaiian Salt: Made by adding activated charcoal to sea salt, black Hawaiian salt is known for its strong flavor, and is often described as "earthy." Sprinkle it on finished dishes. We are all works in progress, and as we finish our journey and return to the earth and dust, our soul, with all its lessons, learns and moves on to be sprinkled onto finished pieces of our journey.

10. Smoked Salt: We create smoked salt by cold smoking salt with wood (such as alder, apple, hickory, or mesquite) for up to two weeks. Get smokin'! Don't be afraid if your life gets a little heated and oily. Through the embers of the fire, you will see renewal.

11. Himalayan Black Salt: Also known as *kala namak* (which means "black salt" in Nepalese), this reddish-brown salt is created by cooking rock salt with charcoal, herbs, seeds, and bark in a furnace for twenty-four hours. Black salt is the opposite of white table salt and can bring intrigue and inspiration to the table.

12. Pickling Salt: Used only for pickling, this coarse salt contains no iodine, minerals, or caking agents. Don't get caught in a pickle, especially with pickled salt, because too much will render your dream pruned and dry.

Amazing, right? I'll bet that you have never considered just how many types of salt there are and the different functions, uses, and, of course, flavor profiles for each. There are so many options to enjoy. But it doesn't end with just seasoning. Salt is essential to our health. Much of the salt that we need is naturally present in most foods, such as meat and seafood.

Salt is found everywhere. Some animals, however, such as horses and cattle, require access to salt blocks, and wild mammals and birds are known to gather at natural mineral deposits to ingest the sodium they need for survival. It's wise to use salt sparingly at first and then taste your way to the perfect amount. The same holds true in life, as you determine your building blocks along the way. Use wisdom, growth, and experience to learn and grow.

But salt is not just present in food. It's everywhere in our lives - in the ground, in the sea, in the air and is essential in our bodies. But a correct balance of salt is necessary to maintain good health. Low levels of salt can induce nausea, muscle cramps and dizziness, caused by low blood pressure, whereas too much salt raises your blood pressure and can lead to heart disease and stroke.

Nature remarkably allows us to regulate proper salt levels. Consider sweating for example. Salt is a major component in our sweat and after strenuous exercise, the release of excess salt normalizes our body temperature. We also cry salty tears—an emotional release. When we swim in the ocean, its salt content helps us heal as we relax, take stock, and rejuvenate. Salt is buoyant and helps support us.

As you can see, salt serves as a cornerstone of our lives. It can normalize the mistakes we make, and we can learn from them. For example, salt can represent a failure that hurts. But it only hurts because we're learning the hard way. Salt in a wound hurts, but it also cleans and heals. Salt can be your bad attitude and can attract bad experiences. Use less salt and improve your attitude. Salt can also represent your feelings. In short, salt is everywhere. It's everything. It's unavoidable in cooking and in life. If you live, then you live with salt.

Salty Hardships

Often salt has a give-and-take property. Salt can at times act as a metaphor for life's unpleasant events, seen in many of the clichés that we often experience. But as darkness is to light, salt can demonstrate the difference between the good times and bad. Salt, in many ways, helps us better understand the sweet. Without salt, we wouldn't have a point of reference. However, as we further unpack the role that salt plays in our lives, we can begin to see that salt, while seemingly unpleasant at first, is a crucial part of our very existence.

Here are some of the more popular sayings involving salt:

"Give neither counsel nor salt till you are asked for it." This means that you should solve your own problems before minding other people's. In this proverb, salt is the catalyst for change. But it's always best to wait until you are asked for guidance before offering advice. This can lead to discord. Instead, learn to listen. Hearing exactly what people have to offer is a true skill. Listen and you will find messages that you need to hear.

"Salt in the wound." We have all heard this one. It generally indicates the idea of adding insult to injury by rubbing salt into an open wound. This act makes the unpleasant situation worse, often reminding you of your failures or faults. It really hurts, but on a closer look, through the pain, is a healing effect. It's good to feel the pain, as it helps you to learn and grow. Salt offers you emotional calluses so you can withstand pain, be stronger, and learn and grow faster from future failures, so you can get on with things and not let the pain deter you.

"Salt of the earth." This refers to a very good and honest person. If you are truthful with yourself, then you can be responsible for your decisions and choices. This is the fastest route to arriving at the best you and, therefore, the best life, or you may choose to lead a shallow life with no meaning, always on the lookout for the next person to take advantage of.

"With a grain of salt." This means to view something with skepticism or to not interpret it literally. Salt is like judging and criticism. This leads to insecurity, doubt, and low self-esteem. You can only help others by sharing the salt that you have used to better your life.

As you can see, salt in our lives is simply unavoidable. Even if we don't actively think about it, we experience it every single day in one way or another. Salt is hardship. But that doesn't necessarily mean that it leads to a negative experience.

In fact, hardships help us explore our weaknesses. They help us develop empathy for others. They help us appreciate our lives, health, and friendships. When we learn from them, we inevitably grow as we stop repeating them. Hardships keep us real, meaning that, when we get "too big for our britches," they give us insight into our character, who we are and where we are in our lives. Are we exposing a positive or a negative side of our character? The learning we gain through our hardships act as benchmarks for our success. Are there still lessons to learn? Or have we already learned them?

Hardship pushes us to our limits and, while testing our ability and resilience, it allows us to heal after experiencing life's struggles. How you choose to act, react, or handle unpleasant situations can teach you a lot about who you are and how you view the world. Have you learned how to become the best version of yourself? Have you let adversity, such as death, loss, sadness, and/or anger dictate who you are and how you will behave in your life?

Hardships increase your awareness of the blessings you have in your life. Experiencing gratitude will likely attract what you are really searching for. For me, my greatest hardships, and their resulting pain, have always led me toward power and strength. The tenacity I experience each time I get knocked down leads to opportunities to not only grow but to soar and inspire others around me. The more salt in my life, the better my life often becomes. That is not by coincidence. For me, there is a very meaningful and real connection between salt and success.

In many ways, salt is our greatest teacher. We don't know what hardships are going to teach us but, nevertheless, they are the tools of learning. As Les Brown says, "Every setback is a set up for a comeback!" Life is too short to continue making wrong choices and bad decisions. A friend of mine lost his license because of drinking and driving and spent six months in prison as a result. Some would think his prison experience was a waste of time, but without that experience he would have continued to mess up his life. He used six months of his life for self-reflection and a burning desire to say, "I never want this again." He has gone on to have children and become a successful business owner. He is now dedicating his life to helping others and teaching them about kindness, love, and the power of forgiveness.

Hardships are integral ingredients in life, like eggs to an omelette. In order to fulfill dreams and goals, you need to experience mistakes and failures. Without *hardships* you will never have the opportunity to test your limits and see what you are truly capable of. As you endure problems and pain, you progress towards overcoming hardship. Just be prepared for the possibility of confusion and anxiety that failure may produce. *Hardships* aren't proof that your ambitions are futile or that you should give up because you are on the wrong path. It has been said that "everything looks like a failure in the middle." You can't make soup without getting the kitchen messy. Although a rocket may not make it directly to the moon, it does eventually arrive, by continually making mistakes and correcting them along the way.

Remember this adage, "Progress often masquerades as trouble." The people around you may withdraw their support and be critical of your efforts, and you may start doubting yourself. This is when all the "best is on the other side of fear!" Don't give up! Failure belongs here; it's a sign of progress. The safety net of the status quo may seduce you down toward it, but the struggle and pain are what give you strength, just as weights in a gym help you to develop muscles (Ouch!).

The Salt of Life

You've heard this slogan but think about its relevance: "*Salt* sustains and enriches life." *Salt*, although often taken for granted, is pivotal to our society. It was so valuable that, at one time, it was used as payment for work done, as in "He's worth his salt!" Perhaps *salt* can represent not only your *progress*, a building block toward becoming who you are, and allowing you to reach further and achieve more, but also your wisdom, experience and knowledge that allow you to create your life/soup.

Whether it's in cooking or in life, we all know *salt*. While we may view a *salty* experience as an unpleasant hardship that should be avoided at all costs, in truth, *salt* really enhances our lives, just as when we are cooking our *soup*. We use *salt* for all of its *versatility*. Sure, at times we experience just a little too much of it, such as when we oversalt the soup but if we use just the right amount, *salt* is an amazing enhancer. In fact, the more often that you experience *salt* in your life, the stronger, more able, and appreciative you will be.

We learn from *salty* experiences. Be patient as well as courageous and turn your terrors into triumphs. Have a "when one door closes, another one opens" attitude. Accept that life is not always fair, but that it's mostly balanced. Keep moving forward, have faith in yourself and others, and, in turn, you will create more light at the end of the tunnel. Accept change in your life, as it often shows up to create better opportunities. Add *salt* when you need it, remove it when you don't. Learn from past *soups* and past *experiences*. *Salt* is essentially a *foundational* ingredient. We can't overstate the history of *salt* and its importance in our progress as a civilization.

Hippocrates was the first of many to encourage his fellow healers to immerse their patients in seawater to heal various ailments. Today we use *salt* to *heal*. We also use it to add flavor to our soup and to our lives. We use it as a point of reference. It's everywhere, a vital part of our very existence. It's within us. It's all around us. *Salt*, like anything else in life, is a *tool*, as an enhancer for a chef and also as a guideline for each of us. We need to keep reminding ourselves that *salt* helps us bring *balance* to our lives. *Precision* is the key to creating a *balanced* approach to the pursuit of our goals and dreams. We are all *works in progress* facing boundless opportunities. Let's discover them!

CHAPTER 5

A PINCH OF ROCK BOTTOM:
HOW I REBOUNDED, AND YOU CAN TOO

> *Rock bottom will teach you the lessons that mountaintops never will.*
>
> –Unknown

At some point we have all hit *rock bottom*, feeling like we have been submerged in total darkness. Our mental well-being, as well as our body, reverberates with *fight-or-flight* emotions. Our cortisol level rises, and we feel ourselves sinking into an abyss of discomfort. It's normal to feel this way after a huge blow. Accept the fall with the understanding that tumbling down the rabbit hole is just a temporary lapse before you start over again. The thud of hitting rock bottom is part of our existence. How we face these challenges defines how high we can soar. Just as in life, the preparation of our soup can offer us some of the same obstacles and hurdles.

In cooking, you may end up ruining your soup and after all your hard work it tastes terrible! As your family forces the soup down, they politely state that they like it, but you know it's not true and you will have no choice but to put it in the garbage. That might seem frustrating but starting fresh offers you a wonderful opportunity to get it right, to make sure your soup recipe, or your life, is better than it was before you found yourself at rock bottom. Now is the time to get up and fight back! Put forward some unusual moves, ones that may appear to contradict common sense. Unconventional success calls for unconventional wisdom and action, not common ones. Sadly, most of us will choose to follow the obvious course of action. We fall into the habit of relying on what has worked best for us in the past. We become attached to the *usual* because we have learned that it's safer, less scary. New methods feel insecure, awkward, and risky.

Remember that, even though something may have worked for you or for others in the past, sooner or later, they may not. Sure, it's more comfortable and safer maintaining the status quo, but if you have your sights set on far higher levels of success, *safe thinking* will do nothing for you and your most reliable actions may become major obstacles to your future success.

Climbing out of the abyss will provide you with a clear idea of what *not* to do. You now have the opportunity to improve on your recipe. When a soup is not turning out right, you empty the pot and start again. At that point, you feel that nothing can be done to turn your soup into what you want it to be. You screwed up but you know that you can handle it. It may be an issue of too much or too little or the combination of everything put together. It's time to empower yourself and start over.

As you begin again, you feel uncomfortable, but the trick is to use this feeling as a stimulant to follow *new patterns* of thought and action, realizing that more of the same will yield only the same disappointment. The *try harder trap* doesn't work, simply because, sooner or later, you reach the point where you can't try any harder. And what do we call that? *Rock bottom*! We're wiped out, used up, feeling discarded and exhausted with nothing left to lose or gain. *Rock bottom*!

Rock Bottom

On the plus side, *rock bottom* offers us the opportunity to use this condition as a *reset button*. The previous plan didn't work. Now, let's gather ourselves and try again. There are two options: 1) remain where we are, or: 2) learn from our mistakes. Some people give up and stay at *rock bottom* for years. They allow that moment to replay over and over, keeping them stuck in the mud. But how do we bounce back from *rock bottom*? We need to start with an abundant feeling of *gratitude* for *everything* that we have and engage in *enriching* activities, such as proper breathing, meditation, connecting with the source, and experiencing the joy of nature. All of this will engender a positive perspective and an all-around readiness to move forward.

Hitting *rock bottom* is the final hurdle that you face after you fail. In my case, you may be thinking, "Big deal! She forgot some music, hurt her foot, and struggled through a triathlon...!" Well, what if I were to tell you that, before any of that happened, I had gone from an affluent, upper-middle-class family to being a homeless teen, then a single mother cleaning toilets and hotel rooms to make ends meet, while I literally carried my daughter with me in a papoose throughout every job, all the while worrying about where I'd get her next diaper or bottle of milk? That is my truth, my *rock bottom* story.

My home life deteriorated after my mother re-married, and I had to live with a verbally and emotionally abusive mother and stepfather. I had to escape and, eventually, without a stable support system, I had no choice but to hit the streets at the tender age of 15. I tried to continue going to school, as I was raised to believe that school was the only place to make anything out of myself, but outside of school, I spent my time scoping out safe spots to lay my head down for the night. Consider how scary it was for me to try to find a safe place to sleep every night. I bounced around, just trying to keep myself afloat. I lived in and out of girls' homes, but that came with its own set of horrors. Then, when I became pregnant, the stakes got even higher, and I knew that I had to do something. I knew I wasn't to blame for my situation but wallowing in self-pity wasn't going to sustain me and I had to act. I had to do something, because the thought of being homeless again, pregnant, and on my own was the worst that could happen. I knew I had to move out of my *rock bottom*. If and when you reach your rock bottom, you too must move outside of your comfort zone because only then can you begin to claw your way back out and reach some form of comfort and relief.

Bad Day, New Start

Have you ever had a really bad day? I'm not talking about 'a stubbing-your-toe' kind of bad day. I'm talking about a bad day that has a domino effect, where one bad thing after another happens. These are such painful days that they sometimes feel never-ending. We have all been there. Nothing seems to go right, from your morning coffee order to hitting your head on your desk when you drop your stapler. And then your boss doesn't like the big pitch that you spent the entire week cultivating. Then you sit in two hours of traffic, only to get home to a pile of dirty dishes and your kids needing help with their calculus homework. Yikes! This may sound like a terrible set of circumstances. But perhaps compare your day to someone who just found out a loved one was diagnosed with cancer, or someone else who barely survived a car accident. It's all about perspective. Your *rock bottom*, and the feelings it provokes, are yours. You own them. Although they may seem insignificant in relation to those of others, to you they are real and now you must deal with them!

You won't fully appreciate the joy of the *highs* in your life without having experienced along the way the disappointment of the *lows*. Highs and lows not only complement one another, they also remind us of just how sweet and sour life can be, just like the old sayings of give and take and yin and yang that bring us back to the notion of establishing and maintaining *balance* in our lives and with our soups.

When I spoke of *balance* in the last chapter, I focused mostly on *neutral* feelings. Now let's consider *extremes*. Some things that happen to you during your life will be categorically *BAD*. No doubt about it. You will experience loss, grief, pain, and sadness. They are such an unfortunate part of life. However, when you have that first *good* experience after feeling something *bad*, you feel *relieved*. This makes feeling *good* all the better because you know what *bad* feels like. Such as hitting *rock bottom*, a point at which you think that *it can't get any worse*, or that *it's only up from here*. That's when it's time to rise up from the depths! However, getting yourself out of that rut without suffering is impossible; there will be suffering. But use this bad time to discover what you can do to improve your situation. You need to ask yourself: "What do I need to do to be better? To feel happy again? How am I going to shake myself up to reset and recharge my life?" Make your million-dollar soup and think deeply about what you want to accomplish this time around.

Rock Bottom and Others

Life is a choice. When we focus on intuition, emotion, love, and friendship, we learn the importance of strong connections, community, and collaboration. But when we fail to focus on these strengthening elements, our foundation may easily collapse, causing us to make bad choices and spiral downward, out of control. As we try to numb out reality and ignore our pain and suffering, our problems instensify and make matters worse. Our relationships and our jobs deteriorate because we don't follow the rules. We develop a bad work ethic, lose our self-respect, self-esteem, and self-worth. Unfortunately, bad situations can often arise in life, and lead to failure, and, ultimately, to *rock bottom*.

Many things may cause this to happen to us. Do you see that unfortunate fellow standing on the corner begging for change? He has most likely hit *rock bottom*. Drugs, alcohol, finances, grief, and even boredom or a loss of perspective can drag you down into this state that feels different for everyone. For me, it felt like a whale had swallowed me and that I was sitting in the dark abyss of its belly with a huge gaping hole in my heart. Struggling with this feeling of despair and isolation, I drew more deeply into myself, searching for a desperate hope that the hole in my heart could be filled once again, this time with light, joy, laughter, and freedom. Playing the piano saved my life so many times as an inspiration that picked me up, as I allowed the music to transport me. Creative activities such as dancing, painting, baking, cooking, and writing all have healing properties that can initiate and speed our recovery.

Rock bottom is an essential part of life. We can't escape it, no matter how hard we try. When it occurs, we can either dwell on it and stay stuck, unable to break away from the failure, or we can learn from it and move on. Nothing should stop us from persevering, from attempting to move on in life by developing a different approach. When we hit *rock bottom*, we can't give up and wallow in it. Instead, we need to search for a way out, perhaps by learning from the recovery strategies that were successful for others. Chefs always taste their own food, as well as that of others, just to make certain that they are on the right track. Recognizing what we have or don't have can help us arrive at realizations that will encourage us to aim higher and grow in the process.

There will always be someone around you who is really struggling, and in greater pain than you are. I don't say this to minimize your feelings, but rather to remind you that perspective is key in solving your problems and your challenges. If others can survive great loss, pain, and suffering, you can too! Remember that it's never as bad as it appears or feels. Life is what you make of it. It's all about choices, and how you react to your circumstances. Life is 10% what happens to you, while 90% is how you react to it. So how do you plan to react?

Sometimes hitting *rock bottom* is not always something that you feel; sometimes you feel nothing. For example, as I mentioned earlier, I experienced a traumatic childhood that eventually led to very dark times. I started out as a good child from a good family, at least until I was relocated and forced to live in an abusive environment. Before long, I was forced to couch surf, and when I ran out of couches, I stayed wherever I could, until my last resort was to hit the streets. I reached my lowest ebb one night while the cold and continuous rain was pelting through the slats of the bench under which I was curled up. Instead of feeling any emotion at all, I felt none. There wasn't anything left in me to feel. I was *numb*. But it was that *numbness* that changed my life that night. I had come to a crossroads, and my choices were to *give up* or *get up*. I decided to *get up*, and although it wasn't easy, I made my way through it and, in time, I became an educated and successful individual. I often think about all the other ways it could have gone. Many unsavory characters traveled around me, and if I didn't have a good head on my shoulders, I could have faltered uncontrollably! Thankfully I didn't. In my case, numbness gave way to an urgent need for survival and made me realize what I had to do. I needed to create a steadfast and effective course of action with priorities that would lead me out of the dark and into the light. I decided to discover what life had to offer and, at that point, I became determined to rise up from *rock bottom* into the *sunshine*.

Rebuilding from the Ground Up

In life, the challenge is not only recognizing that you have hit *rock bottom*, but also moving out of it. Although you may feel that your life is hopeless and that you have exhausted all options, being there allows you to see the bigger picture. It all comes down to having *hope*, a four-letter word that can literally move mountains! *Hope* allows you to pick yourself up and be glad that you did. Two things are certain: you will never forget being there and you will also remember how you got up again.

We all have the ability to determine what we want from our lives and where we see it going. The first step toward creating that new life is knowing where you want to head. Would you just throw a bunch of items in a pot and hope for the best? Not likely, so, if we plan something as simple as making soup, why wouldn't we focus on planning something as important as the rest of our lives? Certainly, our lives deserve careful thought and planning! Again, ask yourself what you dreamed of as a child and what keeps coming back to you time after time. This is your mind reminding you to follow your purpose. If you really work at it, you will discover where you are headed, and even though things may change along the way, you can always have an end goal in mind.

We can all agree that no one wants to be unhappy, and when we reach our own *rock bottom*, we are definitely not happy! Who wants to be down and out? Of course, it feels better to be happy and doing well. When you hit *rock bottom*, rebounding can be as simple as making new choices, looking at other options, and then making changes. This is the time to ask people for help. Kind people are everywhere—family, friends, strangers, whoever, but be ready for the challenges that you will be facing and be strong enough to believe in your plan no matter what. Let the people in your life know what you want and why it's important to you. They may be able to help. But don't use others as a crutch because there is only so much that they can do for you. *You* must be the one to exact the ultimate change in your life, and a lot of it can start with your mindset and your purpose.

Focus on that energy, the positive and the good that exist every day. If it's a horrible day, *focus* on the sound of birds that you hear as you walk down the street, or give someone a pleasant smile so that you can receive one back. Another difference maker is helping others. Doing it for the mere joy of helping them, without expecting anything in return, will give you satisfaction. "Do unto others as you would have them do unto you" is an adage that can help you create a life of closer interaction and self satisfaction. The universal laws are always at work, and it makes sense that we should reap what we sow. When you strive to give others a helping hand, let the world open to you and give you a life of generosity and fulfillment.

As difficult as it may sound, try to come to terms with your *rock bottom*. When things are not going your way, remind yourself that "this too shall pass." The less you allow it to impact your life, the less it will. It may not be your choice to find yourself here, but you can choose how to respond. *Rock bottom* can last hours, days, weeks, years, or forever. That is ultimately your choice. Be open to the process and remember that it only takes one step at a time to begin to move upward from the bottom. Imagine yourself submerged in deep water, looking up toward the surface. You instinctively think of your safety and immediately pull and kick as hard as you can to the air above the surface. Do you remember my simile for "flower salt?" Be limitless, like the ocean, and know that all of that infinite space ahead of you can be yours, if you keep in mind that this is where you will discover your whole new life.

Let's view *rock bottom* from a different perspective. Consider the skyscraper, or any other large building. It requires a solid footing to stand tall and firm. So, you know who strive to hit *rock bottom*? Architects, construction workers, engineers. Anyone trying to build a large, spectacular structure needs to hit *rock bottom* in order to establish a firm foundation! Every architectural wonder in our world had to hit *rock bottom* before it could be constructed upward.

So now what? Are you ready to welcome new failures as a bridge toward a defining moment that will change your life? Maybe you already have failures that you can look back on to create a deeper awareness that will act as a catalyst for your transformation and growth. If not, go ahead and shoot for the big prize and live a life of being different by staying true to your own needs and desires and embracing a perpetual state of surrender and faith. You can decide to abandon the status quo and be yourself. Think about the impossible and ignore the usual. Change your behavior and set new patterns!

Now is the perfect time to rely on your intuition to guide you. Say goodbye to your *rock bottom*! Upward and onward! It's time to break out of your self-imposed prison of perceived constraints. Think NO LIMITS! Forget about what you *think* you can have or what is possible and begin to go for it! Allow your beliefs to become probabilities. Dream! Risk! Be free! Act as though you have already succeeded.

CHAPTER 6

THREE CUPS OF STRENGTH AND A DASH OF EMPATHY:
PERSEVERANCE, DETERMINATION, AND ENDURANCE

> *The world breaks everyone, and afterward, some are strong at the broken places.*
>
> – Ernest Hemingway

The Japanese have a beautiful art called "Kintsugi." It involves putting broken pottery pieces back together with gold and is built on the idea that, in embracing flaws and imperfections, you can create a stronger, more beautiful piece of art. I believe that this artform is nearly as beautiful as the potential for beauty that awaits people who are reconstructing the broken pieces of their lives.

If a crushing blow of adversity ever has you down and out on the ground, bruised, and battered, remember that you are good enough, that you can survive. Sure, it's challenging, especially in those moments, to find the perspective and inspiration to forge ahead and recover. So how can you respond to adversity? My answer is through *perseverance, determination, and endurance* which I refer to as the three cups of strength and a dash of empathy. By following these tenets, you will discover the resilience that you need in order to face challenges and truly overcome.

Strength is the ability to see your way out when everything has crumbled around you. It's easy to think positively when everything is going well, but it requires a great deal of strength and motivation to think positively when everything around you is not going well. Viktor Frankl, a respected neurologist, and Holocaust survivor, avowed that, despite the extreme physical and emotional torture he endured in the concentration camps, the Nazis could not take away his thoughts and beliefs. Having a strong will encourages you to focus on what you need to do, despite the serious adversity that exists around you. Imagine using a magnifying glass to catch the sun. It lights the paper on fire. The same concept applies to your will and ability to overcome adversity. Use it like a magnifying glass and point it in the proper direction. Do that and you are on your way.

Recently I met a woman in her mid-thirties who told me how much she still misses her mother who passed away over fifteen years ago. She just can't get along without her. This poor woman expresses how she is unable to cope without her to the point that she rarely works and even the smallest problem has become an insurmountable obstacle. She has lost fifteen years of her life grieving, unable to heal and get over her loss. If only she could realize that her mother would want her to let her go and get on with living life. This is just one example of how *a lack of strength* can allow past challenges to stop us dead in our tracks and how we need *to summon strength* in order to bounce back.

The concept of *strength* differs according to our life experiences. Sometimes we need our physical *strength* when the body is under duress. At other times it's the *strength* of our mind, or our mental health, that can lend strength to the body. Many people struggle with this and spend years searching for a solution, either by striving to find their purpose or to recognize their inborn abilities. Sadly, the woman I mention above is slowly wasting away, both in mind and body, as she succumbs to her grief over the loss of her mother. This situation not only affects her but also those who love her, making them feel sad and helpless.

I have known many wonderful people who, despite being extremely intelligent, are unable to succeed in their day-to-day living. Even though they understand what they need to do to remain in control, they struggle. As someone who had to find her strength at a very early age, I don't remember a time when I didn't feel strong. But that's not true for everyone. I have watched people stumble their way into sickness, disease, and depression, too weak-minded to handle much at all. Although some may find their footing, others don't and end up wasting their lives by living in the past. Still others need to endure terrible emotional pain before they develop the strength to survive and thrive. Our thoughts play a pivotal role in how we engage in our everyday experiences. I have seen people *misthink* their way into illness because they are unable to calm the overwhelming negativity that clogs their brains, their hearts, and, ultimately, their whole existence.

This is where our million-dollar soup comes into play. When we make chicken noodle soup, we usually use carrots, noodles, and chicken - ingredients that combine well. Without them, we would be left with little flavor or sustenance. The same is true in life. But instead of carrots, noodles, and chicken, we need to combine *perseverance, endurance,* and *determination.*

One more secret ingredient wraps up the whole process - *empathy.* A dash of *empathy* goes a long way. Add this to the mix and *you* are on your way. *Empathy* is the glue that bonds us together and fosters community and good will. When we treat others from an empathetic perspective, we extend a caring vibe that instills strength and courage that they may have lacked before. Being there for others reflects your worth as a compassionate person.

But the journey may be long and difficult. When I look around me, I'm gratified to see that, despite this slow climb upward, the trek often remains steady and fills me with the hope that we will make it. Our pace doesn't matter if we always keep moving and improving. *Strength* is not something that comes naturally to us. As with any skill, we must develop it. It's a condition that we craft for ourselves, not something that we are born with.

Strength Overcomes Adversity

Strength inspires us to try again. We may fail over and over, but, as we begin to learn from our mistakes, we recover more and more quickly. That is *strength*. It motivates us to discover what we need to do in order to prevent ourselves from ever being in a hopeless situation again. Gaining *strength* teaches us to be resourceful and gather insights that allow us to reach our goals. Inner *strength* keeps us looking forward, not back, nor to relive our past mistakes and failures. *Always onward and upward!*

Nothing could have prepared me for my early years of struggle. But those years are what helped me to prepare for anything that would come along. We can't succeed without *strength*; it's that simple! Those who truly live need to be strong to get through life, which is not always going to be perfect or easy. We can anticipate things becoming difficult and then even more difficult. These are the times that we need to prepare for if we expect to stay above water long enough to survive the storm. There is always something new to discover when we keep our heads above water.

The First Cup: Perseverance

We achieve *perseverance* when we possess the sheer willpower to follow through, achieve our goals and be successful in life. It provides the means to overcome obstacles that hinder us from reaching our destinations. *Strength* gives us a clear, confident outlook in the face of opposition, as we push onward with determination and persistence towards our goals.

We have all heard the saying, "Where there's a will, there's a way." In other words, when you *persevere*, you find a way, or you create another way despite the obstacles. Eventually you reach your goal. I love how water slaps against a rock, but then it flows effortlessly around it. So much in life takes the *path of least resistance…* water, electricity, wind, and, too often, we humans. In his famous book *Siddhartha*, Hermann Hesse describes the fluidity and amazing path of water: "Have you also learned that secret from the river; that there is no such thing as time? That the river is everywhere at the same time, at the source and at the mouth, at the waterfall, at the ferry, at the current, in the ocean and in the mountains, everywhere and that the present only exists for it, not the shadow of the past nor the shadow of the future."

Taking the *path of least resistance* can happen if we rationalize things, deny truths, or distract ourselves. Imagine what we could do, though, if we decided to change our outlook, rather than take this easy path. Instead, why not make the harder choice and put in more effort to reach a decision that will bring us closer to achieving our goals? People look at *effort* in individual ways. What is relevant is that it's important for us to make an *effort* to control our thoughts and work towards maintaining consistency and balance. As creators of our destiny, we need to be in control.

Perseverance means having the determination to arrive at a chosen destination, no matter what. It means there is hope because you are confident that your *effort* will improve your chances of reaching your goal. When you *persevere*, you create achievable possibilities in life. Successful people persevere and gain, even with the small stuff.

Perseverance means not giving up. You need to stay strong to persevere. You will be facing challenging obstacles, especially when you are pursuing a worthy goal. It takes a lot of courage to maintain the determination to see something through! There will be people telling you that you can't, people who don't believe in you, even people who would rather see you fail. Ignoring the disbelievers and being determined not to fail will increase your inner strength. If you pay attention to what others think, you will become distracted and lose confidence and control of your thoughts and priorities. Never lose sight of the fact that we are stronger than we believe. As humans, we can adapt, even under uncomfortable circumstances. "Nobody said that it would be easy!" We need to be open to continuous learning, growth, and toughness in order to reach our dreams. Why be satisfied with *mediocrity* when, with *perseverance* and *effort* we can succeed? Together, let's dream, learn, teach one another, and do the things that we are passionate about so that, along the way, we can develop our *strength*, and our ability to *persevere*!

Perseverance prevents you from falling by the wayside when setbacks occur. Keep forging ahead, in the face of all odds. Once you reach some level of success, you will become more confident that you can achieve more. *Perseverance* is like a rocket heading toward its target. It sets a course and is always shifting to right itself. Maxwell Maltz was a surgeon who coined the term "Psycho-Cybernetics," which refers to "steering your mind toward a productive, useful goal in order to reach the greatest port in the world, peace of mind."

We can't have *perseverance* without *strength*. The two together create a powerful duo that enables us to conquer obstacles as we maintain a clear focus on reaching our goals.

The Second Cup: Determination

Determination means that you are willing to do anything to achieve your goals, no matter how challenging. When you act with *determination*, a clearer vision of your goal will become evident, and you will know what steps to take to achieve it. It's the eyesight of your goals and provides you with the awareness and understanding of what you desire.

Determination also helps you remain focused while you are working toward realizing your dream. It's inevitable that outside influences will come into play. You will hear well-meaning loved ones, friends, even strangers telling you that you should give it up. They may make fun of you, and even insist that you don't know what you're doing. Take it *all* with a grain of salt. *You are not the sum of their thoughts; you are the sum of your own!* You are you, and you create who you are. There is no place for naysayers along the way. I enjoy it when people say: "It's none of my business what other people think!" I taught this notion to my three daughters and many others when they found themselves in frustrating predicaments. It always empowered them to stick to their plan, no matter what!

Determination will keep your mind stoked and you strong in the face of adversity. I'm a very *determined* person! Why? Because I'm so obsessed with my dreams that I will never give up. I'm *determined* to reach the end of my life fulfilled, and I strive every day to work on molding my life in such a way that the end goals come to fruition. *Determination* allows me to *persevere* and feel, with certainty, that nothing can stop me.

Goal setting with *determination* will leave you feeling so galvanized that when you reach each goal, your confidence will soar. This *strength* then becomes your character. This is when life really becomes interesting, and you realize that you hold the power to lead by example and help others in their quest.

This transformation is powerful, because when authenticity becomes the core of your character, you become a leader. You will have won, becoming your own *chief chef,* sharing your remarkable million-dollar soup with others, since you will have learned to give as well as to receive.

The Third Cup: Endurance

Endurance is steadfastly holding out for the long haul. You are "in it to win it." Using your *determination* and *perseverance* over time will allow you to build *endurance.* It's like a muscle that you work to strengthen each time that you exercise. *Endurance* increases your ability to live life *lock, stock, and barrel.*

When life gets messy, and it will, *strength* and *endurance* will give you the confidence to deal with the obstacles in ways that will lead to success. With *endurance,* you will have a measure of resilience to help you weather the tough times. Your *endurance* will allow you to maintain mental stamina and self-confidence. You can do this by thinking positively. Visualization is another technique for handling stress and developing mental toughness will help you create the *endurance* that will sustain you as life goes on. Learning a hobby and practicing every day also tests your *endurance* and allows you to measure just how far you are willing to go.

Music is my passion. When I sit down to play, I know that my endless *endurance* and devotion to mastering the piano enabled me to play beautiful music at the touch of my fingertips. The journey to reach that point was rigorous, often requiring intensive practice morning, noon, and night to achieve the requisite skill and precision. I have to admit that it definitely tested my *strength*. Thank goodness I didn't quit! These days, sitting down at the piano is one of my most joyous pastimes.

The more that you *endure*, the better will be your ability to handle hardships and stress for an extended period. I'm a long-distance runner (but I didn't start out this way as I was a sprinter in my youth), and it's not possible to be successful at this without significant stamina. *Endurance* takes time, a lot of effort and both perseverance and determination to maximize your strength and reach your potential. Furthermore, the memory of each success builds upon whatever *strength* you need to guide you to more successes.

How does putting these three cups of *perseverance, determination,* and *endurance* together intensify your strength? The answer is that, all together, these components make it possible for you to become the best version of yourself, a superhero. You can have or do anything. You will always know how to find what you need. Napoleon Hill, an American self-help author who is best known for his book "Think and Grow Rich" (1937) said, "The will to the mind is like steel to carbon. Alone, the will is nothing. Add it to carbon, it's indestructible."

These three ingredients will make you *indestructible*. You become as strong as a tardigrade, a microscopic, eight-legged animal that is known to survive under the most devastating circumstances. They are the most indestructible animals on earth and can survive up to thirty years without food, live in volcanoes, and enter the vacuum of space. Having control of the three ingredients is akin to wearing a full-body, bullet-proof suit. Just like a superhero, your strength accompanies you everywhere you go, in everything you do, and with everyone you meet. Trust me, if you keep your eyes open, you will begin to realize just how strong you can be.

This combination—*perseverance, determination,* and *endurance*—makes you feel that anything is possible. So, look for these traits in people who have done amazing things. Study and emulate them, and soon you will be the example for everyone around you.

Three cups. That's all it takes. They are sitting right on the counter next to you and are ready to become part of your soup. Add them in, let them enhance the soup and then immerse yourself in wonderful feelings as life gives you all that you deserve.

CHAPTER 7

DON'T FORGET TO STIR:
MOTION CREATES SUCCESSFUL STABILITY

Just keep stirring the pot; you never know what will come up.

– Lee Atwater

Motion is the simple act of transferring energy from one place to another. As dancer Martha Graham said, "All that is important is this one moment in movement. Make the moment important, vital, and worth living. Do not let it slip away unnoticed and unused." This simple but powerful quote reminds us that, whether we are making our million-dollar soup or improving our lives, *motion* is *action*. It's the medium through which we create change, transfer energy, and apply the subtle force that alters the very existence of one thing or another. *Motion* opens doors. It unlocks the potential for opportunity, the pathway to success, and adds more roads to meaningful change. While *motion* may appear to be unstable, it actually works to create remarkable *stability*. We move to feel peaceful, to build up and break down barriers to be all that we can be. We were born to extend ourselves and expand our souls and minds. Expansion creates extensive opportunities and puts us in touch with more people, which in turn fosters community.

While we are making soup, one of the most basic and nurturing actions that we do is stir the ingredients in the pot, using constant and subtle movement to blend the flavors. Motion, in life, creates energy, momentum, and motivation. When we are in *motion*, we don't settle and become inert. If we remain immobile and inactive, we don't serve our best selves, our highest interests, or our uppermost goals. Ignored soup is not good soup.

To achieve the best results in life, you need to be in a constant state of change (motion) because, if nothing changes, your results won't change either. When you lose momentum, you may procrastinate and begin to doubt yourself. This can cause you to lose sight of your *why*, as well as the action steps that you intended to take to reach your goals.

Stirring allows you to move toward important goals. It redistributes the heat more effectively and allows you to reignite your passion and even create new solutions, products, and procedures, which increase the rate at which we redistribute the heat, creating a buzz of activity and fresh results. Once things have heated up, you may reduce the heat and stir less frequently, as long as you don't forget to stir. The same holds true with movement in life. As Sam Levenson, American television host, journalist and writer once said, "Don't watch the clock; do what it does. Keep going."

As long as we make a concerted effort to keep moving, we leave open the wonderful opportunity to reach our highest and most coveted goals. The second that we stop moving, we effectively give up on what really matters to us. Think about yourself as a baby, unable to move. Babies are stationary, without any strength or knowledge of how to crawl, walk, or run. But as they develop and grow, something wonderful happens: – a sense of motion. Babies begin slowly, first rolling over, and soon afterwards, they learn how to crawl. Then, over time, they take off. The world is their oyster, with so many places to explore. In many ways, they can't be stopped. Eventually, they take their first steps, and their parents celebrate. Why? Because they realize that their children are beginning to unlock the doors to opportunity. Now that they are moving, they will grow and begin to chase their dreams.

Oddly enough, and perhaps, sadly enough, as we grow, we may abandon our sense of motion. We move less and remain motionless in front of computers, phones, and other devices. We forget when, at the very start of our lives, movement was celebrated and listed on a pedestal as our most important goal. It's crucial to note that *movement* is often the pathway to a nurtured and prosperous life.

A long, healthy life is no accident. In his *New York Times* bestselling book, *Blue Zones*, author, and longevity expert, Dan Buettner, draws on his research from extraordinarily long-lived communities around the globe, or Blue Zones, as he calls them, to highlight their lifestyle, diet, outlook, and stress-coping practices which add years to their life and life to their years.

A long life begins with good genes, but it also depends on good habits. If you adopt the right lifestyle, experts say, chances are that you may live up to a decade longer. So, what is the formula for success? Longevity, Buettner has found, is deeply intertwined with community, lifestyle, and spirituality. You won't find *longevity* in a bottle of diet pills or with hormone therapy. You will find it by embracing a few simple but powerful habits and by surrounding yourself with the right people. Your tribe is your vibe, like the perfect ingredients for your soup. Mingling with certain people will open the doors to opportunities you didn't know existed, just like adding a new spice to your soup may cause a fusion of taste that you have never imagined.

It's then no surprise that the first and maybe, the most important, step that you can take to live a long life is to *keep moving*. Buettner goes on to state that the world's longest-lived people don't pump iron, run marathons, or join gyms (not that those aren't worthwhile goals/practices, by the way!). Instead, they live in environments that require them to move automatically without thinking about it. They grow gardens without modern conveniences for yard work. Therefore, if we are to survive and live, we have to move.

Motion doesn't just shift physical presence and energy. It also creates *emotion*. Mixing your body or your ingredients means changing your mental state. This will potentially enable you to break negative patterns and make room for more positive ones. *Movement* is one of the keys to becoming unstuck. As we move, our bodies release *endorphins*, or happy chemicals, that change how we think and feel. *Movement* leads to creative expression and happiness. I carried out one of my biggest challenges and dares when I dove from an airplane. You can join me here: janet-lynn.com/jump. That was one of the biggest movements that I have ever imposed on both my body and psyche. Wow! That indescribable feeling of adrenaline surging through every cell in my body was like a Ferrari racing and coursing through every vein in my body. I wonder how exhilarating it must feel to be a race car driver. That kind of *movement* takes practice, precision, and a pure understanding that will get you through the unknown every day.

Movement with Others

As we have touched on, *stirring* allows flavors to share their uniqueness with other flavors, thereby creating the best blending of tastes. Also remember, as you move toward your goals and ultimate dreams, you need others to blend into your experience and help you along the way. You can accomplish this by finding people with similar mindsets, attitudes, and backgrounds to collaborate and share ideas with you.

Some people call this a *mastermind*. It's like someone performing a magic trick. Whenever we work and move forward, the unexpected appears. Ideas come to us and solutions to problems become clear. At times, combining our strengths and sharing our weaknesses create synergies, producing a unified effect that can often be far greater than the sum of their separate effects. Together we can do so much more. Let's never forget how community can help us thrive. Bees know this well, and Mother Nature reminds us of this with the pure, sweet honey that the bees provide because of their community work.

Stirring Offers Us Perspective

In addition to *moving* us toward achieving our goals, *stirring* gives us a valuable dose of *perspective* and *insight* into our lives. It creates *movement* that provides endless options and opportunities as we move into a new dimension in our life! Here we can taste our creation as we make an accurate assessment of its true fundamental flavor. In doing so, we may find that we need a little bit more of this or a little bit more of that. That's adding *perspective* which *balances* the flavor, adds dimension to our life and ensures that we are performing at our best.

Let's consider the association between *movement* and our *health*, an area that has been seriously *underrated*, and in the scheme of things, hugely *undervalued*. In fact, movement is vital to improving our health which requires both a regimen of proper *nutrition* and *exercise*. Joining a gym or, more simply, going for walks with friends, in either sense, can do the trick. As is the case with any new endeavor to start, it's not all or nothing. You need to start slowly, a few minutes here and there. Then, as you gain *perspective* and *insight* into your health, and become stronger, you can put more effort into your exercising, thus increasing your *movement* as you work towards developing your own *stability* and *balance*. The same holds true while you are in the process of creating your million-dollar soup.

Movement Creates Stability

We have already learned that *effort* creates the *movement* required to reach *stability* and *balance* in our lives, as we continue to strive to reach our goals in meaningful and fulfilling ways.

Stability, as it relates to the overall success of our personal lives, helps to keep us *grounded* by keeping us on the right track. We develop a plan and create well-thought-out and intentional action steps that fit into our vision and keep us on course. When we are *unstable*, we become *unorganize*d, which leads to doing things that take us off course. We need to maintain our *focus* so that, if we begin to go off course, we can easily find our way back. *Stability* of the mind and spirit is essential to our goal of achieving concrete success. Being *unstable* leads to disappointments and inconsistencies.

Professional success and emotional well-being are characterized by appropriate and well-thought-out decisions that are consistent with our life goals. When we are in control, we feel *stable* and *balanced* and therefore, are much more likely to experience *satisfaction* with integral aspects of our life. When others see this, they know whether to come closer or stay away, as our aura and energy increase around us, exuding confidence and stability that make any naysayers disappear into irrelevance.

When you consciously create your life by *stirring* and staying in *motion*, you have less drama and fewer unnecessary problems to deal with. You have decided to no longer allow your life to knock you around and, instead, you are in control by experiencing confidence, pride, and satisfaction. So many around us who are struggling are often going through life with no plan, no purpose. They make poor choices and flit from one situation and/or relationship to another. Every area of their life is affected, including: unhealthy diet, erratic sleep patterns, failed relationships, lack of motion, and lack of healthy emotion. Generally, they are just down in the dumps and miserable.

They experience emotional highs and lows and are on the lookout for the next best *temporary thing* that they hope will make them happy but, most likely, it will lead them further away from what they truly want. This is where addiction and substance abuse come into play, to help numb the pain. Again, knowing what you want out of life is the key to unlocking your *potential* and working towards what you propose to be and do.

Having *stability* and control of your life enables you to influence your behavior. So, when you feel that things aren't going quite your way, how can you regain the *control* that you need? Ask yourself what you are hoping to achieve, and whether or not you are missing something or need to change anything.

Look for ways to reach *stability* and take charge. Don't just allow life to happen to you; you must *make* it happen. Only you can make the appropriate choices, based on what your goals and dreams are. Create a routine that includes all of the steps that you need to take to be successful. For instance, if you want to save money, eat healthy, and have quality time with your family, you must plan out what you need to do each day to achieve those goals. Perhaps you want to make soup with your children. You'll need to plan a trip to the grocery store, buy the right ingredients, and schedule the time you will need to make it together. When you include activities in your day that help you get closer to your goal, you feel that you have accomplished something. And this will give you motivation to become more and more committed and organized.

A word of caution regarding lists. Most of us believe that we are moving forward as we clutch our never-ending to-do lists and tell ourselves that *achieving* means having all of the list items crossed off. But is that really what *achieving* is? Have you ever questioned how checking off list items is helping you to move forward? Perhaps you may feel a modicum of satisfaction, but this is just temporary, because tomorrow you will invariably add more, and even more the next day, and the day after that. Yes, you are in *motion*, you're doing something, you are heading somewhere, but are you moving in the *right direction*? What is your ultimate *destination*? If this sounds familiar, as something that you have struggled with, I strongly suggest that you make certain that your checklist meets your needs and that you are following the recipe that will allow you to make your million-dollar life soup.

We need to strive toward developing a sense of happiness and fulfillment in what we are providing, especially if we can feel that our most rewarding work is what we do for others. Don't we admire people who receive a lot of satisfaction from what they are doing, such as mothers with three, small children who just love being with them, doctors who go out of their way to tend to their patients, teachers who stay after school to help their students? These providers only see the good that they are doing and the benefits that they are gifting their children, patients, and students.

John Wooden, an outstanding UCLA basketball coach, never really thought coaching was his highest calling. However, it became the conduit for him to have an impact on people but, in the final analysis, he needed more *movement* in his life to keep him *stable*. What did he do after all of those practices, games, and national championships? In his spare time, he could be found sweeping his own gym floor. With all of the resources in the world, there was Coach Wooden staying up late and sweeping the UCLA gym court. Why? Well, can we suppose that this extra *movement* helped calm him, helped provide strategies for improving his team's results with a better game plan and also decrease his obsessing over the "X's" and "O's", necessary to lead his team to success? He realized that one must do the little things in order to make an impact. Find your broom and move. Your life needs movement, and *motion* is the path to *opportunity*.

CHAPTER 8

TWO TABLESPOONS OF POSITIVE THINKING:
THE WORLD REWARDS CONFIDENCE

A man cannot be comfortable without his own approval.

– Mark Twain

Our *mindset* is the greatest *ingredient* at our disposal. And a *positive mindset* will facilitate *success*. Although we all aspire to think positively, it's not always easy to do. Negative thoughts and bad habits can get in the way. Few of us want to be negative, but we all face forces that sometimes stir up negativity and drag us down.

Do you know the story of Eeyore who always portrayed the "poor me" donkey in the Winnie the Pooh series? Well, we have all encountered Eeyores in our lives, people who, by concentrating only on the negative, are perpetually miserable and pessimistic. They expect the worst to happen, no matter what the face of reality may look like. They don't seem to change; it's as though they are addicted to feeling that way, with often detrimental results. Some people, believe it or not, are addicted to sadness, mayhem, and even disaster.

There is no doubt that it's difficult to break any habit, and more so, a bad one. When we are feeling down, we tend to surround ourselves with people who are also unhappy and not living their best life. While it's completely normal to experience these periods of negativity, we need to pull ourselves out of them by becoming positive and hopeful that better days will come.

We need to tell ourselves to stop being negative and force ourselves to feel grateful and appreciate the good things in life. The quote: "stop and smell the roses" can change our day. This is an abbreviation of the original quote from golfer Walter Hagen in his 1956 book *The Walter Hagen Story* where he said: "you're only here for a short visit. Don't hurry. Don't worry. And be sure to smell the flowers along the way." Let's try it. We can start by smelling the sweet aroma of our soup and allow it to help push us forward.

Life is a journey along which you alone decide exactly what you want, and how to obtain it. But in order to achieve that goal, you must make the effort to move forward in a positive way. When problems arise, choose not to wallow in them, but instead, look for a way around them in any way possible - through them, over them, or under them. Very little can deter anyone with a fully positive attitude. The most influential leaders of our time adopt an unflinching determination to reach their goals. They move forward with the confidence of knowing that they will be successful. Think about the mother who lifts a car to free her trapped child. How does she do it? By knowing implicitly that there is no alternative, that this is her last resort. Have you ever noticed that, when you want something with all your heart, you simply go out and make it happen? You rarely stop to think about the how or the why. You are emotionally attached to the outcome, and therefore you chase after it.

Practicing *positive thinking* every day helps to build meaningful relationships, as you become less critical of others and the world around you and better equipped to deal with stress and adversity. You will find yourself living life in a more constructive way. *Positive thinking* will also keep you moving forward, building momentum, and embracing new ideas and possibilities. People who associate with other positive-minded people can create more opportunities for themselves as they foster relationships, friendships, and good feelings among the people around them.

Conversely, *negative thinking* is counterproductive and self-defeating. *Negative thinkers* don't create positive results, which leads to frustration, stress, and anxiety. *Positive thinking* encourages you to stay hopeful and appreciate what is, and what can be down the road. The absence of hope is despair, a prevalent emotion in today's world. If you happen to find yourself in a bad state, make the effort to examine your circumstance from a different perspective and search for a positive thread. The "light at the end of the tunnel" may only be a small glimmer of hope but your *positive outlook* will help you to recover your *motion* forward.

Here is a story about a man who goes up to his mentor/coach and says: "I want to be the best writer in the world." The coach says: "I can help you with that. Let's meet out by the water." So, they meet, and they start walking out into the water. The coach stops and asks him: "Do you still want to be the best writer?" The man says he does. "Okay, follow me." They get waist high, and the coach stops and asks him the same question. The man replies: "Yes, but I need you to know I can't swim." The coach tells him to continue following him. They get as high as their necks in the water, and again the coach stops and asks if the young man still wants to be the best. The man replies: "Yes, I do, but I don't know if I can still do this." They continue and go underwater for a short time, then come up and go down, and up again once more. The coach stops and asks him the same question one last time. The man replies: "Yes, I do, but…". The coach then stops him and explains that he will never reach his goal until his desire to do so is so strong that he feels he can no longer breathe.

The point of the story demonstrates that the power of *positive thinking* is like *breathing*. Breathing life into your goal will help you enforce what you need as you live day by day, increasing your ability to achieve whatever you need on the way to that goal.

Positivity Makes for a Great Soup

Initiative, *creativity*, and *resourcefulness* occur when you develop a *positive mindset*, setting you up to be prepared to take on any challenge. When you are putting together your million-dollar soup, taste it many times to determine if you have created a wonderful, enjoyable flavor profile. The better it gets, the more confident and positive you will feel about the outcome. This is the same with your life. As you go about creating your life and interacting with others, they will provide feedback that will help you improve your ultimate outcome. Embrace the mindset of what you can give to the world as opposed to focusing on what the world can give you.

Your brain is naturally wired to take in all the positivity around you! It will begin free flowing with ideas, and you may even notice a rush of endorphins that can make you feel happier and more excited. Like a garden in search of water and sun, your mind is always ready to soak up positive vibes. The more joyful and positive you feel, the more you will boost your confidence and become more resilient when life throws you its curveballs. Remember, the more you live in the present and consciously create your life in a positive way, the less affected you will be by the inevitable bumps in the road. Random events are less likely to bring negativity into your life when you are *positive* and continue designing your life by setting goals and setting out to achieve them each and every day.

They say that the best ingredient in soup is the simple act of love, the careful attention and thought that goes into crafting a tasty and wonderful experience. Love is nothing more than a dose of positivity. And it sure tastes good! *Positivity* makes for a great soup and a great life. It overcomes the humdrum flavors that might otherwise creep into your soup and your life. Have you ever been sick with a bad cold and someone you love makes you a pot of chicken noodle soup? Wasn't it the most delicious soup you have ever tasted? Could it be attributed to the large dose of "love" that went into making it?

Positivity will keep you from getting caught up in a cycle of negative thoughts and behaviors drenched in pessimism. Do you want a different life? Job? Relationship? Situation? If so, transform your thoughts into positivity and renew your awareness of everyone and everything in your life with love and appreciation, and, before you know it, your life will unfold in the most beautiful way.

In my life, when I begin any task, I become more positive and joyful, and, in turn, my quality of life improves. For example, the first time I found out I was going to be a mom, I had no idea how anything was going to work out. I just knew that things would! I was filled with hope and love for this new life that I was going to have, and positive thoughts filled me. It didn't seem to matter that I had never changed a diaper, or that I was single, and had just been laid off from my job. I imagined all the amazing things that would happen in our future. Many people were pessimistic, asking me how I was going to manage as a single mom. A positive mindset was all I really had, and I decided to fill up my cup with optimism. What an incredible adventure being a single mom was for me and my firstborn daughter!

Choosing to live with *positivity* helps you appreciate what you have. There is an expression that says: "It's never so bad that it couldn't be worse." That sort of negative thinking may just make things worse for you. Before that happens, you need to get out of your rut and change your attitude. My husband's paternal grandmother was a wise and incredible woman. She never had a negative thing to say about anyone or anything for as long as I knew her. Everyone called her "Nan" and wanted to be around her. She died at 101, happy, healthy, and knowing that she was well loved and appreciated. She taught me, very early on, the power of *positivity*. Find the *good* in what you have and build on it. By creating a solid foundation with positive thoughts, you are likely to enjoy good experiences.

Just think about what can happen without *positivity* in your life or in your soup. *Negativity* can only lead you to unhappiness and it's a difficult attitude to change. It makes you feel like a failure, and you end up resisting change. Even when friends and family encourage you, your thinking remains rigid and static, recognizing only the problems and, not the joys, in your life. And so, the cycle continues, and you attract more *negativity* and become even more overwhelmed. *Pessimistic* views about life, paranoiac thoughts and constant struggles are common in negative behavior. Negative people who have been this way for a number of years may have come to believe that their outlook is a *normal* way of thinking, as just a part of who they are. In addition, negative people often associate with like-minded people, and this interaction can be quite detrimental. As William James, an American philosopher and psychologist, reminds us: "The greatest discovery of my generation is that human beings can change the quality of their lives by changing the attitudes of their minds." The trick is in finding ways to overcome *negativism* by replacing it with a beneficial, *positive* outlook.

Sculpting a Positive Life

Most people would prefer to take a positive attitude and go through life with a healthy mindset. Everyone's journey to happiness will likely be unique, but we all need to find effective ways to overcome the challenges, if we hope to succeed.

I've stated before that our success isn't dependent on other people's failures. We can succeed without taking from someone else; we can create our own success. We can live with people who are failing and continue to succeed. We are the creators of our own lives. However, there are people who are afraid to fail, so they don't take any risks. They stay in their lane and leave good opportunities by the wayside. It's easier for them to stay comfortable in their failures, rather than strive to change their circumstances. For some people, it's all about *ego*, as they allow their negative mindsets to control their direction in life.

Our experiences often create barriers to our achieving future success. For example, individuals with an unhappy or abusive childhood may never heal, which keeps them from achieving. They live with low self-esteem, even if they are well-educated or extremely talented in other areas. To succeed, we need self-confidence. Believing in ourselves leads to accomplishment, whereas lacking confidence can lead to setting inappropriate goals that produce mediocre results. We need to stretch our limits by confidently and wholeheartedly jumping in with both feet, and never be afraid.

Positivity and *confidence* go hand-in-hand. *Confidence* is the result of *positivity*. Although you may enjoy some success while having a negative attitude, it won't last, since you lack a vital *foundation* for long-lasting achievement - a *positive* and *confident* outlook on life. *Success* is the outcome of nurturing *positivity* and *confidence*. So, the more positivity you gain from yourself and the people in your life, the more confident you become. This will encourage you to take more risks and, in turn, achieve your goals.

Positivity is found at the heart of *optimism*. Successful people are confident that their plans, abilities, and efforts will allow them to reach their goals. Even though a positive self-image is largely developed in early life, it can be changed by replacing self-defeating thoughts and habits with a positive, optimistic, confident outlook.

Have you ever noticed that confident individuals adopt an "I can't lose" attitude? They seem to be superhuman, soaring above everyone else. They have no doubt that what they set out to do will work out. If obstacles do show up, they adapt and find ways around them. Thus, they continue to thrive, no matter what they have to face. A positive attitude, along with confidence and high self-esteem, leads to feeling whole and healthy. As you grow in self-awareness and develop self-confidence, you will exude positivity in all areas of your life.

With the aim of crafting a positive narrative for our lives, we must first take the essential steps to support a *foundation* for success. Our habits, our lifestyle, our gratitude, and thankfulness for all that we have are all key indicators of our success. When we surround ourselves with like-minded, *positive* people, we believe in ourselves and move in the right direction, taking impactful steps that support our success. We can continue advancing toward our goals by making a list of 5 significant goals that we have reached and for which we are *grateful*. Then we can choose 5 that are on our wish list and that we are eager to achieve. That's our *positivity* confirming that we are able and willing, and have the confidence to do it, which, in turn, provides us with the momentum and subsequent *motion*.

Learn to accept yourself and come to terms with who you are. What are your strengths and weaknesses? Ask yourself if you would like to change, and if so, how. Are your desired changes congruent with your values and beliefs? How do others perceive you? Some of us know ourselves well and accept where we are in our journeys thus far, and then there are others who know, but purposefully disregard their shortcomings, preferring, instead, to foolishly believe that they are better than they are. This may lead to disaster, if they decide to turn to alcohol or drugs in a futile effort to bury their failings.

If you are struggling with accepting yourself as you are, make certain that you aren't comparing yourself to others. When you do this, you may compare yourself in a *negative* way, so remember to give yourself a break. Each of us is unique and equipped with our own distinct strengths and weaknesses. Forgive yourself and move on, not allowing the past to bite you in the backside. Believe in yourself.

The world rewards positivity and confidence. We see this time and time again. If you are confident, you will be living your purpose and attracting people and opportunities into your life. You will have a magnetism of sorts. People will want to follow you, be around you, and establish meaningful friendships and relationships with you. Just as when you serve a delicious soup, people will want to be given the recipe.

The world acknowledges *confidence* by taking notice, offering awards, and celebrating achievements. Numerous prizes are given to top performers in fields ranging from sports to politics to science to writing. They are all meant to highlight and celebrate individuals who have ascended to the top of their field. I recently learned that I had been a finalist in the "Next Generation Indie Book Awards" for my fiction book, "Forever Is Today." Learning this filled me with a sense of satisfaction and excitement to begin a new project, reigniting my *purpose* of being an author.

Creating Your Positive Life

Armed with the knowledge that *positivity* will fuel *success*, we can now start to sculpt a more positive, impactful life. An ideal way to begin this is to focus on living in *the present*. Stop spending time thinking about the past and reliving emotions that have no value in the *present* or *future*. Replace old habits of *negative* thinking with new *positive* ones. Look for the good in everyone around you and find some joy in every moment. Have you noticed that the most highly successful people are also some of the happiest? Think about successful businesses. Are the people at the top confident and happy? Maybe not always, but most likely they are happier than the workers at the bottom of the ladder. Also "don't sweat the small stuff!"

I will never forget the moment the doctors told me that my 15-year-old daughter was a very sick girl and would likely need a liver transplant, since she had less than 7% of her liver function, due to autoimmune hepatitis. My mind immediately filled with images of losing my daughter, planning her funeral, and wondering how I would continue to live without her. I knew should that happen, there would be no way I could ever breathe again. I was making plans to check myself into the nearest psych ward and just give up on life and waste away.

Sometime later, my shock changed to anger, and I directed it towards everyone in my path. I blamed myself, asking why I didn't notice her symptoms before. I questioned if somehow, I caused this. *Was it something I did unknowingly while I was pregnant?* This progressed into feelings of devastation and loss, and I soon found myself in a state of complete *sorrow*. I'm not a crier; I can count on my fingers the number of times that I have cried as an adult. But there I was, sobbing on the floor of the hospital as I desperately pleaded with God, or the universe, or anyone, to spare my little girl and take me instead. But I soon got hold of myself and realized that I did have some *control* here. I could *control* how I *thought*, so I began to think positively about her situation. Perhaps the medications and procedures would work. Maybe a new medication or therapy would be developed to cure her. And, if all else was lost, she would be one of the blessed few who would be selected to receive a liver transplant. Well, here we are five years later, at the time of this writing, and although life has forever changed for her and our family, we think positively and deal with life one day at a time, filled with hope. My daughter is now following Dr. Joe Dispenza, bestselling author, and famous lecturer on neuroscience and quantum physics, and is on a journey to heal her body.

Two years ago, I wrote a novel based on my daughter's life. It's called "Forever Is Today" and is and is being shopped in Hollywood! We are in the process of creating *The Gilbert Foundation*, an organization to raise money and awareness for autoimmune liver disease. We have been asked to speak at events through the liver foundation. My daughter and I are co-writing a children's book about the harmful effects of alcohol and drugs on the body and how to keep your liver healthy. I'm also in the process of establishing a support group for parents living with sick, young, and adult, children. None of this would be possible, if I hadn't turned my initial *negativity* into permanent *positivity*.

The point that I'm emphasizing here is that, when you are dealing with potential life-changing events, it's up to you, and you alone, to determine whether or not you want to remain *miserable* or do something *constructive*. The responsibility is yours, resting on your shoulders. There is no doubt that life will test you, as it tested me. That is just part of the journey. But nonetheless, we are each empowered to create a positive and self-serving life, despite what negative events befall us. We must overcome the urge to remain buried in our *negativity* and prepare ourselves to move toward *positive change*.

The first step toward introducing *positivity* into your life is to decide to change your *attitude*. It's not easy, and it takes practice. As I have previously touched on, it involves surrounding yourself with *positive* people; *negative* people can pull you right back down. If you have *negative* relationships, distance yourself from them, until you have managed to make being *positive* an everyday mindset. Read material on having a positive attitude and keep it close. Avoid looking back on your "report card." Your future is not based on your past. When you were tested and failed, that was then. You must create a new *today* that is not based on yesterday's information. Look forward to new, better times. The wake at the back of a boat follows the boat, not the other way around. Always remember that your future is not dependent on your past. Disassociate yourself from it and embrace new and rewarding life events. Create enthusiasm to obtain the results that you want. The only purpose that your past has is to allow you to focus on your wins and gloss over your losses.

Concentrate on replacing your *negative mindset* with *positive action*. Today is a new day and it directs you to where you are to go tomorrow. Ask yourself what you would say to someone else and think about what you would want that person to say to you. Likely it would be: "Keep trying." Use this idea to reframe your situation. As negative thoughts creep in, think about all of the positive ways that things can turn out. Drop everything that is negative and find people, interests and activities that will reinforce your desire to move out of the dark and back into the light as soon as you possibly can.

More than any other possession, our mind is the key to overall success and our likelihood of reaching ideal outcomes. The mind creates and maintains a positive outlook and takes this perspective even further by increasing our confidence and ability to *always* use that mindset through thick and thin. Our mind is indispensable, the most valuable ingredient for our life and our million-dollar soup.

Positivity is a mindset, and one within which we should all focus our thoughts and feelings. Armed with a positive mindset, we will find it easier to navigate challenges, overcome obstacles, and manifest the best version of our life. The world around us is our resource for rewarding our positivity. It's a powerful magnet, attracting the best that we can imagine.

CHAPTER 9

KEEP STIRRING:
NOTHING COMES EASILY

*If you really want to do something, you'll find a way.
If you don't, you'll find an excuse.*

– Jim Rohn

Unfortunately, life doesn't amount to a single can of soup resting on the top shelf in your pantry. Life takes time, effort, energy, planning, and, as we explored in Chapter 7, a hearty stir, just as it does for your million-dollar soup. Turn on the heat, and we're cooking. A soup is the culmination of many ingredients and much effort in the hope that it will taste as delicious as we anticipated at the beginning. But keep stirring and keep tasting to balance its bold and enhancing flavors. Too much salt can render a less than optimal outcome. Too much sugar can leave us feeling rather heavy and uncomfortable. Balancing the aromas with consistent flavors is a process that requires work and attention but, in the end, it's most definitely worth the effort. And even more rewarding is the sharing of what we have stirred up with those around us. The

Bob Marley song, "Stir It Up" truly expresses my message, as his words confirm what will give our lives meaning. So, stir it up, "little darling," until the consistency of our lives becomes exactly what we want it to be.

Making our million-dollar soup, as we well know, is a process. It's fine to start by using canned soup, but the goal here is to move forward toward creating an entirely new recipe all on your own. As with everything in life, you start small and move upward. Canned soup is fine as a beginning, but it's uninteresting and bland. There is a saying, "life in a can." I would imagine, that just as canned soup is motionless and congealed, by remaining there, your life would be too. Think outside of the box, give free rein to your dreams and your whole recipe will set you free and allow you to stretch your limits and then share this unique formula with the world. Being stuck in a can would limit your vision and render you motionless. Get out of the can, your rut, and enjoy life to the fullest. Move on and add motion to your soup, and your life. Keep *stirring*!

Life provides us with many *ingredients*, and it's up to us to choose those that can best move us toward reaching our goals. Just as with what we put into our soup; we have control over what we put into our lives. Some of the ingredients, however, are often beyond our control, embedded deeply within us from a very young age, such as the family we are born into and the values we are taught. Use these values to your advantage. If they no longer serve you, change them. If some cause us difficulty, we have the potential to re-shape them by the decisions we make over the years. Although you are born with a certain body, you have the opportunity to treat it according to your preferences. As a child, I remember my father telling me that, when I didn't like what I was given for dinner: "It all goes to the same place." You can mold yourself to become who you want to be. Just live your true nature by stirring things up. But more often than not, the situations that are beyond our control are beneficial as well and can be used as a springboard to achieve higher success. Regardless of your background, you have the power to reach your goals and live the life that you choose, an abundant life with a mix of ingredients that will enhance the flavorful moments throughout your journey.

Don't remain static. Change is not easy, but the greater the challenge, the more satisfying is the reward. Even when the heat is on and something doesn't go your way, or you burn your soup or the flavors are not what you had anticipated, this lets you know that it's time to reflect and reassess.

Although many of the choices we make in life are within us from a very young age, as we get older and reach our own milestones, we can attempt to take control of our future. We are responsible for creating the lives that we want to lead.

So, ask yourself:

1. Is the life that you are living the one that you expected?
2. Is it the one that you want?
3. Are you following through with the steps that will lead you to where you want to go?
4. Do you take time out to think about what you want and who you are?
5. Are you living your life as the person you think you should be, or based on what others think?

6. Have you ever considered that you may have made some wrong decisions in the past? And if so, how do you propose to remedy them?
7. Are you content with remaining where you are?

These are not easy questions to answer. But they are crucial to the direction that you would like your life to take. Sometimes, the life that you are leading is "perfect" for you today, but as time passes, and new events recalibrate your "status quo," life may not be so perfect tomorrow. Consider this example from my own life: I married a sweet, intelligent man when I was twenty-nine. I moved three thousand miles across the country to begin my life with him and become part of his milieu of family and friends. It was a huge change, but it was the one that I wanted and the one that I chose. Over time, without even realizing it, I had unconsciously molded myself into being the woman he and everyone else wanted and expected me to be. It happened. I let it happen. Upon reflection many years later, I realized that I had lost sight of my own goals, aspirations, and personality. I lost me. And I'm not alone. This can happen to the best of us.

I love my new life, being a mom and wife while discovering what it was like to belong to a family again, without having to live in survival mode all of the time as a single mother, never knowing how things would work out or what was going to happen next. So now here I am, suddenly married and settled somewhere with a routine and a dependable living situation. I enjoyed the transformation, as I found purpose and meaning within my little family.

Over the years we had two more children. We added a family dog to the mix and bought a grand home on twenty acres in the rolling hills in rural Ontario. My husband's work took him across the country for six to eight months of the year. Sounds crazy, I know. But the money was fantastic, and we were young and energetic. Our soup spilled over, and abundance, as well as flair, flourished in our household during those years. My life was filled with juggling my daughters' dance lessons, long hikes with Mandy, our dog, baking cookies, field trips, educating my daughters about life, cooking, cleaning, enjoying family time while playing games and watching movies, date nights and all the rest of the details that go along with being a homemaker.

It wasn't until I turned 40 that I began to hear my inner voice telling me that I wasn't living the life that I really wanted. I no longer was the Janet-Lynn who loved to be out in nature, write, play music, and be part of a collective that exuded creative juices. I ignored it for a while. But soon I realized I wanted more. I wanted to create my million-dollar soup, but I didn't have all of the ingredients that I needed to be satisfied with my life while being a Mom. I was missing many of the ingredients that I had hoped to use to fill my life. I had become a one-dimensional character, almost robotic in my daily functioning, a bland, insipid pot of soup with run-of-the-mill ingredients that had no zing. Don't get me wrong! I love my family and would do anything for them, but back then, my soup was lacking. I forgot to add some *passion* to it and forgot the importance of *stirring* it. By allowing this to happen, I had lost a crucial part of myself; I wasn't quenching my thirst for the creativity that I craved.

I realized that I was living like a *can of soup*. I was stifled, as many of my innate abilities remained unexplored. With this realization, I started to get back in touch with who I used to be and wanted to become once again. I re-examined my purpose, my goals in life, all of the things that I truly cared about and went about figuring out the steps to achieve them. I made my list and sharpened the skills that I had temporarily left behind and successfully performed before The Royal Conservatory of Music. I went back to being physically active. I began a rigorous exercise routine, and, along the way, I played soccer and trained for, and participated in, six triathlons. I earned various personal training certificates, as well as my black belt in kickboxing and then opened two kickboxing fitness gyms. And some brand-new passions were ignited in me, a love of writing, public speaking, and a glaring need to inspire others. Now I write daily, have had several speaking engagements and I am on the road to developing new ways to spread my message. My life is forever changed.

Do what you love - The Phrase That Pays

Life is not "a bowl of cherries." Most worthwhile things don't come easily. But don't let that discourage you. The best things in life take time and energy, and they are well worth it. The *ingredients* that make your life *meaningful*, such as your interests, talents, and dreams, need to become *habits*. When you add your chosen *ingredients* to your *life/soup*, be sure to include the ones that have had the most impact on your life. For example, you can say that you have ingredients such as *motivation* and *inspiration*, but what trumps these is *your discipline*. *Discipline* creates *habits*. So, for your *best life/soup*, you need to instill *habits* that promote thoughts of *positivity*, a meaningful *mindset*, a healthy *lifestyle* and so much more. By the end of the day, you will have created your amazing, *million-dollar soup*. Repeat this and you can manifest the same wonderful flavors day in and day out.

But this amazing soup needs you to turn on the heat and constantly stir it up in order to transform what may have begun as an insipid, congealed glob of canned soup into something special. I put the heat on in my life and continue to rev the engine of my soul to stimulate my newfound habits and keep them alive and active. Good habits that have become totally intertwined into how we live our lives are our best friends. I could have remained mired in my bowl of canned soup, but instead, chose to pepper up my life by constantly stirring my soup.

The idea that nothing comes easily in life supports the very notion of hard work. Try not to be like people who perpetually feel sorry for themselves by allowing disappointment and mediocrity to rule their lives. Be that person who forges ahead against all odds and overcomes adversity. Put in the effort required to accomplish your goals, whatever you set out to do. And only then can you truly appreciate all that you have accomplished. It's inevitable that you will experience hardships, but the key is to move forward and extricate yourself from that toxic relationship, or that dead-end job. Don't engage in promoting negative energy. But to do that you will have to re-evaluate your choices. When you accept defeat, you are making a choice to let life control you. That doesn't have to be the case. Make new choices. Plan to re-invent yourself. Do something you love, something you are passionate about, plow through the rough stuff.

Take the highly successful Kentucky Fried Chicken food chain and its founder, Colonel Sanders. His dad died when he was 5. He quit school at 16, married at 18, and joined the army. His wife left him and took their baby with her. He considered his life to be a failure, and at 65 years of age, he decided to commit suicide. But then something magical happened. While he was sitting there, writing his last will and testament, he thought about what a good cook he was. So, he borrowed $87.00 from a friend and fried up some chicken using his "secret" recipe and started selling it door to door. He worked hard and it paid off, all because he was passionate about what he was doing and was enjoying it. At age 88, he had built an empire and was a billionaire. Wow! Ask yourself: "What do I love?" and then do it. You don't even need to know everything all at once. With passion and perseverance, things will fall into place. Start making your *$1,000,000 soup* by selecting your favorite *ingredients* and get *stirring*! Keep that pot alive and simmering, thanks to the fire in your heart and soul. You can never go wrong!

Work Is Power

Hard work empowers you to do remarkable things, a tenet that has been a constant, life-long *inspiration*. Some may consider me stubborn, oppositional, and even defiant at times, as I have always embraced a *bring-it-on* attitude. I welcome hard work and its challenges. When I think back on most of my biggest hardships and failures, they ultimately became my biggest successes and sources of pride. All around me every day, I hear people say: "I can't," "No," "Yeah, right," "As if," "I don't," "Maybe one day," and other self-defeating exclamations of impossibility. Such total *negativity* leads us nowhere. Instead, ask yourself: "Why not?" "When?" And say: "Yes, I can!" Isn't that a lot easier than remaining unhappy and giving up? It may be scarier being that way but, if you remain negative, in the long run, you will waste your potential and never achieve. Instead, embrace the richness that surrounds you. As its definition in the Oxford Languages Dictionary suggests, your life will be in a "state of existing or containing plentiful quantities of something desirable." You can have it all: - confidence, career, success! Anything!

The way that we manifest change and live a life of achievement is to first become aware of our goals. *Awareness* is what light is to a dark room. Believe that you can, have a productive attitude and watch how things start working out for you. There will certainly be some bumps in the road but, with confidence and determination, you will find a way. You must be committed and always follow through. As Theodore Roosevelt pointed out: "Nothing in the world is worth having or worth doing unless it means effort, pain, difficulty. I have never in my life envied a human being who led an easy life. I have envied a great many people who led difficult lives and led them well."

The above words are oh, so powerful. The price of success is being committed to applying the best of yourself to your dream. It will take everything that you have, but if you love your dream, it will be more than worth it. *Work* is power. Luck and circumstances are wonderful, but rarely is the path to success without work. *Work* is *actio*n, and without it you won't go very far. *Action* is the application of *energy*, our driving force. You must drive that force, and the challenges that you face will create opportunities to put positive momentum, growth, and success in place.

Stirring for the Win

Adding *effort* to our life, or our soup, helps us to overcome challenges as it provides energy to move through *resistance*. *Effort* enables us to *persevere* when the going gets tough. Every time we hit an obstacle, let's take a step back to recognize that the *same effort* that we put in to overcome the last struggle will help us to overcome the one that we are now facing.

Navigating a successful life comes down to a willingness to never stop allowing the energy that we create to move us in the proper direction. Be so driven by the thought of reaching your goals that you will be unstoppable. Imagine how you will feel when you succeed and sometimes even pretending that it has already happened can help you in the process. *Energy* will keep you satiated and filled with excitement and hope, which will propel you onward.

There are so many success stories, examples of people who have overcome, despite extreme struggle. Below is a list of some of my favorites:

1. Jim Carrey dropped out of school at 15 to support his family. His dad drove him around to comedy clubs, and before long he began starring in mega blockbusters and became widely known as one of the best comedic actors of our era.

2. A shark bit off Bethany Hamilton's arm while she was surfing. A month later, she got back on her surfboard

and into the same shark-infested waters and became a champion several years later. Hollywood produced the movie "Soul Surfer," based on her story.

3. Publishers rejected Stephen King's first novel thirty times before he got his first deal. Today, his books have sold over 350 million copies and have been made into major motion pictures.

4. Bill Gates, one of the richest people in the world, couldn't make any money at first. His first business failed miserably, but he didn't let that stop him from trying again. The failure spurred him on to success, which is often the case.

5. Albert Einstein didn't speak until he was 4 and everyone took his brilliance as some sort of laziness until they realized "his head was in the clouds" developing the theory of relativity!

6. After Rubin "Hurricane" Carter was jailed for a crime that he didn't commit, he educated himself and never gave up on proving his innocence. Eventually he was released, after spending almost thirty years in prison.

These are just a few of the multitude of astounding changemakers in our society, people who have overcome adversity and developed outstanding lives. These people did whatever they had to do. Examples appear everywhere, not just among the rich and/or famous. In fact, we are all examples of success. We all have a story. Tell it. Put it out there and see what happens. We are all overcoming our pasts and reimagining our future. Your story can inspire others.

Your soup is magic. Everything in it creates a feisty, fiery, passionate, hearty dish that becomes an all-encompassing beacon of lessons through the energy that you invest to create your million-dollar idea. Keep moving, keep flowing, and always be steadfast in the ingredients that you want others to practice in their own lives. Always remain balanced, not too salty, and not too sweet. Be noble and you will see how your soup's beautiful aroma becomes the steam that drives you, as well as the people around you. Soup's up! Let's get stirring!

CHAPTER 10

LEAVE TO SIMMER:
YOU HAVE WHAT YOU NEED; NOW WHAT DO YOU WANT?

Ten years from now, make sure you can say that you chose your life, you didn't settle for it.

— Dr. Anne Brown

Whether we have been making our million-dollar soup or organizing our life, we have all been left to *simmer* in our own pleasures or pains. *Simmering* requires reducing the heat to allow the flavors to meld. It's defined as keeping a food or liquid just below the boiling point while still applying heat. This synergistic process takes time and permits our ingredients to merge, to become the sum of their parts. *Simmering* transforms the ingredients into a blended taste. Let your ingredients *simmer* and you will find your patience rewarded with potent flavors and a wonderful soup.

In life, we often think of *simmering* as negative as it often presents itself in association with anger, and often is interpreted as a state of suppressed emotion or excitement. But *simmering* can also represent something positive. You can simmer on a decision, an outcome, or your feelings. In many ways, the simple, yet important, act of *simmering* can make a constructive difference in how to react to any given situation.

Simmering is action over the long term. It gives our life the time it needs to truly evaluate and commit to a plan, a course, or the journey ahead. If we don't allow the proper amount of time during this process, we may end up with a far less than optimal end product, as in the saying, "Haste makes waste." Act in haste, without simmering, and we will most likely waste our time and our soup will not taste as we hoped. In life, acting in haste is a true conduit for wasted energy and opportunity. *Simmering* properly can optimize our flavors and sharpen our mental faculties, such as intuition, memory, love, will, perception, reason, and imagination.

Although *simmering* serves an important purpose, just as with most things, it also has its limitations. So don't let your soup *simmer* too long. If you allow yourself to overcook it, you will have weakened its flavor. In life, lots of issues can keep us in the pot for too long. One such issue is *fear*, the fear of *failure*, of *loss*, of the *unknown*, and even of *success*. Feelings of *fear* are inevitable. They operate at a subconscious level, making it difficult to cope. *Fear*, if not managed, can paralyze us or at the very least prevent us from being the best that we can be. If *fear* gains ahold of your life, it will affect every aspect of it.

Any manifestation of *fear* can immobilize us, since it undermines our efforts to achieve success. So, when we allow *fear* to interrupt our progress, we miss out on opportunities that would have made it easier to reach our goals. We need the simmer, but not for too long. Imagine how *fear* could have halted many of life's inventions. Would Edison have invented electricity? Would the Wright brothers have built and flown an airplane? And what about important medical discoveries, such as insulin or the polio vaccine?

I wonder how many times Thomas Edison attempted to generate light before he achieved it. Or how many airplanes that didn't fly. Or how many laps Roger Bannister had to run to reach a mile in under four minutes and prove that it was even possible.

We can't evolve if we are gripped by *fear*. We can overcome it by calling on our *confidence, energy,* and *momentum* to take over, calm the *fear* and give us the *courage* and *will* to move forward. However, we won't achieve our highest level of success, if we don't experience at least a modicum of *fear* along the way. After all, what is the worst thing that can happen? We grab a new pot and start a new soup.

Simmering with Awareness

We all want to be happy, find meaning, and be successful. However, we need to show restraint and not start right out with a quick boil. We need to take, instead, a measured approach by going slowly so that the simmering can help us stay focused on detail and quality. We have all heard people talk about speeding up or slowing down. If we slow down in order to take time to consider the details, then, in the long run, we may be able to be more efficient and effectively speed up our activities.

Getting your soup to the right temperature, and allowing it to *simmer,* gives it time to become its best. You have already determined the ingredients to achieve your best soup. In life, *simmering* allows you time to assess, contemplate, modify, and reassess along the way, as you *persevere* with care and moderation. The Oxford Languages Dictionary defines *perseverance* as: "*persistence* in doing something despite difficulty or delay in *achieving success*," whereas it defines *persistence* as: "a firm or *obstinate* continuance in a course of action in spite of difficulty or opposition." A small but indisputable difference.

Obstinate persistence can deceive us into blindly believing that giving up on even a reckless action is unthinkable, thereby leaving us open to the real possibility that continuing with that action could ruin our life. On the other hand, *perseverance* has to do with our overcoming obstacles, purely in order to *achieve the desired results*. Which one sounds better to you?

At one point in my life, I thought that being *obstinate* and *persistent* was of utmost importance in order to achieve my goals. I figured that, if I stuck with something with all of my heart, I would succeed. The proven course of action is *perseverance*, but with the knowledge that we need to be on the lookout for pitfalls, and be especially careful to safely avoid them along the way. By choosing *perseverance*, I felt whole and satisfied, instead of frustrated and defeated.

You may be wondering how to distinguish between the two while navigating through your life. In other words, how do you determine whether you are pursuing *a lost cause*, or working through *a rough patch* that will, at some time in the future, lead to success? If you are *mindlessly* pursuing a cause *simply* for the sake of *persistence* and you are telling yourself that *this time* things will *finally* work out, you need to shift over to *perseverance* and proceed intelligently with a clear, open, and balanced mind.

Don't allow *obstinate persistence* to derail you. Simply find the courage to admit defeat and start over, instead of stubbornly sticking with something that will likely fail. Now is the time to regroup and refocus on trying things a different way. You know that popular definition of insanity: "doing something the same way but expecting a different result." Blind *persistence* causes a lot of frustration and zaps your energy, because you have automatically placed yourself into a "hamster-on-a-wheel" scenario, hoping to see a different result the next time around. It won't happen. Don't be that hamster. Instead of just *persisting*, wisely *persevere* and you will make it to the finish line.

The process of *simmering* will allow the steps to fall into place naturally and smoothly, as you give yourself and your soup the necessary time, attention and care to become what you anticipate.

Simmering Fosters Learning about Inner Peace and Love

Life is a remarkable, wondrous gift, a chance to learn, nurture, and love. However, navigating through life's inevitable obstacles can lead us down dark paths, causing us lots of stress and anxiety. It's too easy to choose *chaos* over *control*. *Simmering* offers you the opportunity to make an informed and proper choice. And this is where *awareness* comes in.

Being *aware* and recognizing what you are putting out into the world is essential to your success, as you will receive back in relation to what you give. We all want to be happy but happiness can come and go in the blink of an eye. *Inner joy and peace*, on the other hand, are created by a feeling of *well-being* that accompanies *achievement, success,* and *caring for others*, as well as our leading a life focusing on abundance rather than on lack.

Simmering Is Growth in Disguise

Some people are *doers* who receive tremendous satisfaction from *creating* and *developing ideas*. But the initial *goal* is the actual *process*, rather than the final *result*. All of this can be exciting and rewarding as they learn who they are becoming and grow with it. For some, it never ends because this is their strength. As they grow, they attract others along the way who assume related roles, allowing everyone to move towards achieving the goals together. Evolving and metamorphosing is a part of nature, and so are we. When we don't adapt and allow ourselves the space to restructure, we remain trapped. So, make certain that you give yourself the time and room to adapt and grow successfully.

Imagine someone, and let's call him Steve, who wants to influence a million people to change the way that they live. He's eager to make them aware of what they want and unwilling to take "no" for an answer. This involves taking risks while they believe in themselves and their purpose. How will Steve achieve this? He shares the down times that he has experienced during his life (bad habits, wrong choices) and takes a new path to create opportunities to attract all of the people and possessions that he wants in his life. He pursues what he wants instead of meandering randomly, as if in a dream. He started small by spreading his ideas and outlook on life to family and friends and then to members at the gym that he co-owns. As the awareness grew outward and spread into his community, people who shared the same views began appearing at his door. Synchronicities and surprises became the norm every day, and his impact began to spread outward into the world. Steve now speaks to large groups of people and mentors young children and teenagers. He is teaching people of all ages to begin thinking and living with purpose. Doesn't that sound awesome?

Many people believe that you need the stars aligned before you can begin to live your dream. Not true. What you need to do is to make the decision to move forward. Add some water to your pot (your purpose), collect your ingredients, (life experiences), and begin creating your own million-dollar soup (your life's aspirations).

The process isn't difficult. However, to be successful, you have to select and blend your best ingredients in order to prepare an irresistible soup, with the intention of serving it to the world. Make certain that this soup is your absolute best! However, don't be concerned if some people don't like it. Not everybody will be enticed by your goal. You can't please everyone, so don't expect to. Instead, gather your people around you, find your vibe, your niche, and grow from there. Every flower started off as a seed, grew and flourished in the garden. So will you. See yourself mingling with the right people at the right time, and the doors of opportunity will open for you.

Life is filled with both joy and misery. It's up to you to decide which one you want to experience more of. The glass is either half-empty, or half-full. It may even be overflowing! At the same time, it's always good to recognize that the glass is not *empty*; at least it has *some* water in it. When the people I love are happy and content, so am I. Life is really an amazing gift that we need to appreciate and enjoy. Of course, at times, life will bring us down, but don't concentrate on how many times that has happened. Remember with pride all of the times that life has tossed you off and you have gotten up, readjusted yourself, and climbed back on. Having inspiring memories to draw on during our down times helps as we navigate through the rough waters and look for the beacon of hope that is out there shining for us.

Simmering Is Dreaming

Have you ever asked yourself these questions? They're important!

1. *Do I have a desire to reach my dreams?*
2. *Do I love my proposed dreams?*
3. *Am I willing and able to sacrifice and go for the long haul?*
4. *Am I willing to fail?*
5. *Am I willing to try again?*
6. *Am I willing to never quit, no matter what happens?*

Nothing can stop you but yourself. The goal never changes. The plan may change; the actions may change. What you want out of life is yours to decide. You have already put it into motion. Keep going in that direction, because, sooner or later, you will arrive. You may discover that it's not just reaching the destination that will be the most rewarding, it's also who you become while you are striving to reach there that counts. Have patience. It's not going to happen all at once. You will need to take the proper steps as you add one ingredient at a time and allow each one to simmer and become the ultimate million-dollar soup.

You must keep *dreaming*! *Dreams* are a magnificent gift! Without them, all is lost. You may find that, without a dream to chase, you will lose interest in life and become bored and complacent. *Dreams* allow you to find a purpose that is essential to achieving success. Once you set your sights on reaching your dreams, you will find the *motivation* to turn your *dreams* into *reality*. *Dreaming* helps you to always strive to improve yourself, to push yourself to go the extra mile. Never give up on your dreams! Follow your passion! The sad truth is that sometimes we don't go the extra mile and, instead, settle for comfort and mediocrity. My suggestion is for you to accept being *uncomfortable*, as this is when all of the magic occurs. Magic is on the other side of fear. I promise!

Dreaming about your goals will change the course of your *entire* life. *Dreams* will set the stage for success by motivating and inspiring you to reach any goal that you have set for yourself. I can assure you that you will never hit the snooze button again, if you keep your *dreams* foremost in your mind. On the other hand, without *dreams* in your life, you will lack the ambition to chase, and have no *goals* to reach. It's impossible to achieve anything in life without goals, and for goals to be set, we need to have *dreams*. Spend time *dreaming*, let your mind run wild, and consider where your life is headed. If you are not actively setting *goals* that are moving in the direction of your *dreams*, there is no better time than now to start *dreaming* again!

Dreaming is at the heart of *simmering*. It's about transforming *thought* into *action*. It's the culmination of the good habits that we have mastered that will lead us to experience joy and fall in love with ourselves and what we have created in our lives. Having the ingredients is not enough. *Natural talent* without effort, energy, and focus, in other words, without effective, guiding habits, often amounts to nothing. You must make the right choices by carefully considering how best to reach your destinations. Appreciate the process. We need to allow ourselves to recharge and re-engage in order to take advantage of the valuable opportunities offered by perspective, time, and the options that lie ahead.

Dream big. The larger the dream, the better the reward. Your life will take an exciting turn, and you will find yourself smiling more and more. I mean, what is more exciting than pursuing one's dream? It's most likely the single most important thing you will ever do because it will be your purpose for being here on this earth. Nobody else will have the same dream as *you*, the same reasons for wanting it. You are unique, so don't allow anything or anyone to slow you down. Life without dreaming big may threaten your chances of success. Don't risk it by remaining just out of reach as you struggle to find meaning and purpose. So, go "for the full nine yards" and do not be satisfied until you win!

Children are born and grow with enormous *dreams*. For them, *dreams* are endless as they develop their extensive imaginations. Unfortunately, their dreams may be extinguished, once they enter the school system where they are pushed to conform. They are instructed to get their "heads out of the clouds" and "pay attention." It's a shame that there are teachers who reproach children who excitedly announce that they want to grow up to be well known, either as rock stars, presidents, or the next astronaut to land on Mars. In our society, children with wild imaginations are often harnessed and brought back down to earth, back to right here and now. As we grow and mature, dreams become the most important goals that we create for ourselves. They become the *why and wherefore* that we feel when we get up in the morning, excited to start a new day. To convert dreams into reality, we need considerable amounts of determination, dedication, self-discipline, and effort. Our dreams should be the stimulation that ignites our soul, as we plan our course of action to make them real and tangible.

Life has an interesting way of flowing by us while we *passively* float along with it. How many times have you heard someone speak of the passing of time? Where did the time go? When we become entrenched in the routines of school, working, and family raising, time slips by without our even noticing. We look forward to future events and holidays, and once they have arrived and quickly passed, creating new memories, we are already thinking about the next item on our bucket list. Don't just let time pass you by unnoticed. Stay aware of the present, pay close attention to who and where you are, and enjoy life to the fullest.

Ask yourself whether or not you are living the life that you always dreamed of. Are you happy? Are you accepting mediocrity? Thoughts such as: "It was good enough for my parents, so it should be good enough for me!" can sneak into our minds, somehow justifying that we need to keep things the same.

Look around at the people you spend the most time with. Are they fulfilled? You may decide to widen your circle of friends and include others who share your mindset. Can you imagine how wonderful it would be to support one another's dreams and share the excitement of moving on together toward your better lives? True success occurs when people collaborate with a united community that strives to ensure the betterment of the whole populace rather than just for themselves.

It's definitely not easy. Because if it were, many more people would be living their dreams and lives to the fullest. Often, we are snared by the monotony of life. Some days are good; some are not. We coast along and accept what life throws our way. Too many of us fail to see that the life we are living just isn't the one that we would choose to live. It may seem reckless to quit a lucrative job to chase a dream, but life improvements result from dreams that succeed. If you are able to dream about doing something, then most likely you also believe that you can make it happen. Albert Einstein has a famous quote: "Imagination is everything. It's the preview to life's coming attractions." Find the *motivation* to live out your *dreams*. Remember that life is short and that, if you wait too long, it may be too late. Keep your eye on the light at the end of the tunnel and ignite yourself with the belief that you can reach any goal that you set your mind on achieving.

Stop and think. That is the gift that *simmering* offers you. Think about what you would really like to get out of life. Too many of us are living idly by, just following the flow of what seems simple, and not focusing on what we really want in order to align our dreams and make them a reality. We often live the life that we believe is expected of us. But is this true? Do people really expect us to live a certain way? I have given this a lot of thought, and I don't believe that this is the case. Instead, we assume that we know what others want from us, and we try to please them or decide that it's fine for now to simply follow the path of least resistance. There is one big problem with this: You only have one life to live, so make the most out of it and do what makes *you* feel joy and fulfillment. None of us wants to come to the end of our life wondering: "What if I had...?"

Think about what you want and why you want it, and then go for it and never stop. Remember that everything you need will appear, even if you can't see it right away. Compare this with how you drive through thick fog when you can barely see in front of you. You keep driving very slowly until you see a little more, and then a little bit more each time. It can be frightening and frustrating, and you will rely on a lot of faith. Let life work *with* you, not *against* you. When you persevere and stay focused, you will reach your destination. The fog will lift and, before long, you will arrive.

Is your fear of failure keeping you from achieving your dreams? If so, convert your negative thoughts into positive ones. Concentrate on moving forward. The trick may be in the thinking, deciding, and then in the burning of the bridge, so that you can't turn back. You must be willing to tolerate ambiguity, confusion, possibly even chaos, to recalibrate your life. Action is the key. In Price Pritchett's book, "You 2" he states: "Look at it this way—you're not supposed to be concerned about what happens in the middle of a jump; you're supposed to be thinking about where you're going to land."

When you take the leap, you may be entering into unfamiliar territory that can't be fully explained. Unseen forces may flow through your subconscious mind and into your dreams, intuition, and good fortune. Use this process as a source of inspiration, a creative solution that occurred to you in a dream, or a breakthrough idea that jumped into your mind while you were driving along in your car. Somehow the resources that you need to put into action may just appear by sheer coincidence. You don't have to do anything more. Just let them happen, without trying to understand them. Just as you don't need to understand electricity to flick on a switch to experience light. As you move ahead, continue to focus your attention on a clear picture of what you are striving to accomplish and approach it confidently and diligently, and the unseen forces will rally to your support.

Too risky? Too uncomfortable? Maybe so, but think about the hidden risks you are up against when you decide to live a life of *mediocrity*. If you *don't go for it*, you will never get what you really want out of life. The sooner that you accept the fact that there will be some risk, the better, because something is always at stake. Whether you choose to take the leap or follow your usual comfortable life, you are putting something on the line. If you hestitate to be a risktaker, wonder carefully if, by continuing to play it safe, you're locking yourself into the surest way *to lose out*.

Let's reframe this. Going for it is simply moving toward an opportunity that you have been ignoring. You are no longer making excuses. You are taking out the pot that has been collecting dust in the cupboard and making a fresh bowl of soup!

Isn't it worth taking a risk on yourself? Believing in yourself? If not, the risk is that you will settle for only a fraction of what life can offer you. And you will be limited to gross globs of gelatinous goop for sustenance.

A lot of people confuse *desiring* with *pursuing*. Their desire for a dream may be desperate and deep, but when that desire fails to produce, they conclude that their dream is unattainable. In fact, though, the only lesson here is that *longing* is not enough. *Pursuit* is what makes all of the difference. *Decide*, *act*, *strive* and *reach*. Only then will life partner with you and help guide you along the way. Leave the safety of merely *wishing* for something and grab your opportunity to *pursue* it.

Simmer, But Not Too Much Heat

Simmering is important to your success, but, like anything, you can overdo it as well. Just as you may overcook your soup, in life, simmering too long is equivalent to taking on too much and trying to speed up the process by going too quickly. Les Brown states: "If you are willing to do what is easy, life will be hard. But if you are willing to do what is hard, life will become easy." This paradox suggests that, when your *why* is strong enough, you will find your *how*.

Sometimes it's good to speed up, but make sure that you keep stirring your life/soup so that it turns out well. By unduly speeding up the process, you may disconnect yourself from your *purpose*. Have you ever tried to suck an ice cube through a straw? It just doesn't work. It will work, however, if you let the ice cube melt first. It's this way with whatever you undertake in your life. You can't just read the book and expect results. First you must read it, absorb and understand it, and then you can apply its lessons. In fact, what about rereading your meaningful books to really let the ideas, words, and concepts simmer away in your mind? You may be successful with some acceleration while you are taking massive action, but only by making very certain beforehand that you have prioritized your actions and that you have a very clear vision of where you are headed. Otherwise, you may find yourself lost, frustrated, and heading for failure.

In "The Strangest Secret," Earl Nightingale gives lots of wonderful examples of how each of us is equipped to direct our lives to achieve success. In one example, he describes driving along the highway and seeing a massive truck with a huge load of dirt. If the driver didn't have a destination or a purpose, he could crash, and flounder and his massive load would be lost. He has all this power in his hands (i.e., steering wheel), just as you have the power in yours. Our minds are under our control. Are you going to direct this power to a specific, worthwhile purpose or do nothing? It's up to you. You are in the driver's seat. People with goals succeed because they know where they are going. A definite *goal* and underlying *purpose* drive them each day as they get closer to achieving their *success*. They clearly understand that, along the road, there will be obstacles to cross or avoid and twists and turns that will require patience and a firm resolve to reach the destination.

Famous American basketball coach John Wooden said, "Be quick, but don't hurry." That thought encompasses the concept of simmering. Slow things down so that you can pause to reflect and ensure that your decisions will serve you in a positive and meaningful way.

CHAPTER 11

NOW WHAT?
LET'S GET COOKING!

Forever is today.

– J.L. Morrison

Now that you have a clear picture of how to make your million-dollar soup, it's time to cook! Time to make your own, unique and delicious soup that will channel all of your creative juices to prepare not just an amazing soup, but also an amazing, meaningful life. Make it the very best that it can be so that you can thoroughly enjoy the leftovers tomorrow, if there are any! After all, your ingredients are delectable and very much worth the time and effort required to produce a satisfying, steaming bowl of goodness right before your eyes. So, sit down and stir up your dream as you let the steam and heat guide you toward success.

Your *million-dollar soup* is not about spending a million dollars, or earning a million dollars, it's about your mindset. It's a mentality, a metaphor upon which to build a meaningful life. It's the means to allow you to achieve what you want, so you can *feel* like a million dollars. This soup is about *you*! It represents your purpose, your goals, what you aspire to. The soup is your segue from ideas to action, to clear the way to achieve happiness and ultimate success. You *are the soup*. But it's a process, not something that can be perfected all at once.

Let's start at the beginning and remember not to rush it. Just as the best things in life take time and energy, so does our million-dollar soup. The foundation of any soup is water, and just as water is a necessity of life, the base of our soup represents our purpose in life, and so, to be successful, we must have a clear idea of where we are going. It's the same with our *million-dollar soup*. Therefore, before you even start cooking, you must identify your purpose, your goal. It must be meaningful to you, something that is vital to your well-being, and will keep you moving in the right direction. Although you may identify many purposes in your life, for the sake of your first million-dollar soup, start with only one. Your soup, like your purpose, will always be evolving. It's a process, but for now, choose that special something that resonates most strongly with you right now.

Next, add your ingredients. I have been experimenting with many soup recipes throughout the different stages in my life, and although they have changed over time, many of them contain some or all of the ingredients that I have listed below. As I realized over time, you may need to mix up the ingredients and make different combinations, or even throw them all away and start from scratch. So don't restrict yourself to only these, and feel free to add any of your own!

It's your soup, your life!

- Adventure
- Ambition
- Athlete
- Author
- Business owner
- Caring
- Compassion
- Competition
- Confidence
- Confusion
- Daring
- Defiance
- Determination
- Disease
- Discovery
- Drive
- Education
- Empathy
- Failure
- Family
- Fear
- Fitness
- Forgiveness
- Friendship
- Gratitude
- Grief
- Grit
- Guilt
- Healing
- Heartache
- Hope
- Joie de vivre
- Joy
- Laughter
- Love
- Marriage
- Meditation
- Motherhood
- Music
- Opposition
- Openness
- Optimism
- Perseverance
- Persistence
- Positivity
- Quirkiness
- Resilience
- Rock bottom
- Sadness
- Sassiness
- Self-awareness
- Speaker
- Sports
- Stubbornness
- Survival
- Sweat
- Sports
- Survival
- Tenacity
- Travel
- Work
- Youth
- Zing

We're not finished yet. We need to ensure the *individuality* of our soup and we do this by adding its own unique flavor that will bring it to the next level, ensuring that it expresses our true nature, our uniqueness. These are your *seasoning*s, the less intangible qualities that may not be as apparent as your ingredients but are nonetheless essential. They add a depth to your soup that your *ingredients* alone cannot. Your soup needs your individuality, your unique flavor, and through your chosen *seasonings*, your soup will express that part of you that makes you, you.

Now mix them all together and turn up the heat, which will give you the *energy* that you will need to activate the remarkable *flavors* and *ingredients* of your *soup/life*. Consider this step as adding a blast of *hope* and *determination* while the delectable flavors ignite and soothe your soul. Bring the heat up to a slow boil, and then lower it, all the while making certain that you keep on stirring. Continuous stirring causes *movement*, a constant intermingling balance of flavors. And, as *balance* is to soup, so it is to life. Now let it simmer to continue to enhance and strengthen its flavors, a step that requires the most time of the entire process. It brings out a new, essential quality called *patience*. You can't simmer and walk away. You must constantly taste it, determine if something needs to be added and then adjust. You will be rewarded with a depth of flavor that you never considered possible by taking the time at this stage. This phase is when things come together, and the magic happens.

As I experienced with my own recipes, they improved over time. My own list of *core ingredients* grew larger as my life unfolded and my true flavors were discovered. I was able to recognize true and rarer ingredients and introduce them lovingly into the fold, just as easily as I discarded others. I am truly grateful for each new discovery, which I was able to adopt into my special recipe, enabling me to become more. I will never stop learning and growing and will remain vigilant for those ingredients that have yet to reveal themselves, as catalysts to my growth. As Robin Sharma said: "Change is hard at first, messy in the middle, and gorgeous at the end!" It's time to grab your pot, pull up those sleeves, and get messy! I look forward to sharing my next recipe with you soon.

Read on and get a few ideas for your own delicious million-dollar soup by coming with me on a journey where I show you how I combined my evolving purposes, different ingredients and seasonings into recipes that created many of my own million-dollar soups, each one being a representation of a certain phase of my life. You will find that some ingredients in my recipes will be sour, some sweet, some bitter, some salty, and some scrumptious, but most of all, they are *real*. From raw ingredients to those succulently cooked, these recipes are a metaphor for my life, in these pages you will find a new world of freshness, vibrancy, and authenticity.

You will notice as you go through each of the recipes that many of them became bigger and better as my life unfolded. My list of *core ingredients* also grew more detailed and I discovered many new and exciting flavors. I'm very grateful for each new discovery, and each new ingredient that was crucial to improving my soup and moving me forward in my life. I will never stop learning and growing and will always look forward to adding new and enticing ingredients for a long time as I move on with my life!

You are hungry and the heat is on. So, let's get cooking!

It's your soup, your life! You've got this!

Good luck and enjoy the ride!

Bon appetit!

Recipe 1

Ingredients:

1 slab laughter
½ cup sports
6 teaspoons travel
1 tablespoon family
4 cups love
¼ teaspoon education
1 cup friendship
1 gallon music
2/3 cup discovery
½ tablespoon failure
water

Cooking Instructions:

Mix together love and family and bring to the boil. Stir in laughter, music, friendship, travel and simmer. Stir in sports, one at a time and add the remaining ingredients, stirring frequently. Add a dash of faith and remain hopeful and patient.

Nutrients per serving:

17% satisfaction, 85% knowledge, 6% happiness.

Tips:

These ingredients were what fulfilled my early childhood, from ages 0 – 10.

Recipe 2

Ingredients:

Core ingredients: laughter, family, love, friendship, music, education, discovery, failure, sports, travel
6 cups fear
2 tablespoons sports
1/2 cup confusion
4 tablespoons sadness
A sprig of hope
1 cup perseverance
A slice of defiance
A pinch of opposition

Cooking Instructions:

Put core ingredients into a large pot of water over medium heat. Add fear, confusion, sadness, and stir in sports. Wait until a rolling boil and using whisk, whip in perseverance and a pinch of opposition. Continue until mixture is hot and then add a slice of defiance and toss in a sprig of hope. This recipe will most likely taste salty and bitter and will need regular additions and subtractions.

Nutrients per serving:

12% discipline, 42% determination, 17% motivation, 2 grams drive, 5 mg energy.

Tips:

These ingredients were what fulfilled my preadolescence and early teen years, from 10 – 16.

Recipe 3

Ingredients:

Core ingredients: laughter, family, love, friendship, music, education, discovery, failure, sports, travel, hope, perseverance, defiance, opposition

Crack 2 servings of grief
One bunch of fear
¼ teaspoon sassiness
1 gallon of heartache
A tub of adventure
2 stalks of grit
A handful of compassion
2 cups illness
½ cup heartbreak
3 tablespoons guilt
A glug of daring
3 teaspoons fitness
A knob of rock bottom
¼ cup sweat
1 cup ambition
½ teaspoon resourcefulness
6 tablespoons determination

Cooking Instructions:

Bring your core ingredients to a fast boil, stirring constantly. Cover and simmer, adding other ingredients one at a time. Be sure to taste often and be careful not to burn your tongue!

Nutrients per serving:

1.5 g desire, 25% health, 60 mg energy, 14.2% satisfaction, 14% motivation

Tips:

These ingredients were what fulfilled my youth, from ages 17 – 24.

Recipe 4

Ingredients
Core ingredients: laughter, family, love, friendship, music, education, discovery, failure, sports, travel, hope, perseverance, defiance, opposition, sassiness, adventure, grit, compassion, daring, fitness, sweat, resourcefulness, determination, ambition
2 bits survival mode
11 glugs motherhood
25 niblets tenacity
¼ cup stubbornness
½ teaspoon resilience
3 ½ cups optimism
A bunch of fear
2 sticks marriage

Cooking Instructions:
Combine core ingredients in pot while marinating motherhood. Spoon mixture of survival mode, tenacity and stubbornness into separate bowl and allow to plump by adding a generous serving of optimism. Return contents of this bowl to pot and marinate together with equal parts fear, marriage, and stubbornness. Next, sprinkle on the ½ teaspoon of resilience, lean back and enjoy the ride.

Nutrients per serving:
2 grams health, 16% determination, 20% knowledge, 16 grams hope, 2% knowledge, 80% satisfaction

Tips:
These ingredients were what fulfilled early adulthood, from ages 25 – 29.

Recipe 5

Ingredients

Core ingredients: laughter, family, love, friendship, music, education, discovery, failure, sports, travel, hope, perseverance, defiance, opposition, sassiness, adventure, grit, compassion, daring, fitness, sweat, resourcefulness, determination, motherhood, tenacity, stubbornness, resilience, optimism, ambition, marriage
22 ½ ounces competition
10 cups forgiveness
2 lbs empathy
½ cup Joie de vivre
3 tablespoons illness
1 slab grief
1 oz tenacity
5 teaspoons resilience
¼ cup athlete
1 slice confidence
2 bunches author
6 handfuls heartbreak
½ cup healing
1 sprig business owner
A pinch speaker

Cooking Instructions:

In a large bowl, mix together all core ingredients. Put 1 slab of grief on a lined cookie sheet and flambé. Crack the bunches of author into a pan and gently baste with a pinch of speaker. In a separate bowl, whip together 1 sprig business owner, a slice of confidence and ¼ cup athlete and, when well blended, transfer to a pot and add core ingredients. Heat the liquid until it's boiling gently and combine the rest of the ingredients together. Season with remaining heartbreak and let simmer.

Nutrients per serving:

85% satisfaction, 20 mg drive, 14% responsibility, 2 grams motivation, 4 mg inspiration, 1% happiness

Tips: These ingredients were what fulfilled my adulthood, from ages 30 – 45

Recipe 6

Ingredients:

Core ingredients: laughter, family, love, friendship, music, education, discovery, failure, sports, travel, hope, perseverance, defiance, opposition, sassiness, adventure, grit, compassion, daring, fitness, sweat, resourcefulness, determination, motherhood, tenacity, stubbornness, resilience, optimism, marriage, speaker, competition, forgiveness, empathy, joie de vivre, ambition, tenacity, resilience, athlete, confidence, author, healing, business owner
2 tubs self-awareness
16 gallons meditation
2 cups business owner x's 2 gyms
1 bunch gratitude

Cooking Instructions:

Combine all ingredients, let simmer, stir often, taste frequently and dish out the contents to the world.

Nutrients per serving:

50% love, 50% gratitude

Tips:

These ingredients were what fulfilled my middle age, from ages 46 – 51.

Dear Reader,

You may have noticed that each of the recipes became bigger and better as they developed. Notice that the list of *core ingredients* also grew larger as life unfolded and the true flavors of my life were discovered. I am very grateful for each new discovery which I was able to adapt to become more. I will never stop learning and growing and will be looking forward to adding new and more rare ingredients as I live my life.

I look forward to sharing my next recipe with you soon!

Janet-Lynn

ABOUT THE AUTHOR

Janet-Lynn, a relentless seeker of life's extraordinary, embraces a single unshakable conviction that has propelled her through astonishing highs and soul-crushing lows, to "live impossibly." Prepare to embark on an exhilarating journey where she unravels the profound power of perseverance, all while holding this very book in your hands. Brace yourself for the art of defying limits, for within the boundless recesses of our minds, the unimaginable manifests itself. With an audacious spirit that challenges the conventional, Janet-Lynn beckons you to delve into the tantalizing realms of 'The Million Dollar Soup.' Unfolding as a mesmerizing metaphor for our very existence, this literary feast awaits to ignite your senses and stir your soul."

Forever is Today - Order now!

Giving a Voice to Creativity!

With every donation, a voice will be given to the creativity that lies within the hearts of our children living with diverse challenges.

By making this difference, children that may not have been given the opportunity to have their Heart Heard will have the freedom to create beautiful works of art and musical creations.

Donate by visiting
HeartstobeHeard.com

We thank you.